THE FRIENDLY HOUR

Tom Jacobson

BROADWAY PLAY PUBLISHING INC
New York
www.broadwayplaypublishing.com
info@broadwayplaypublishing.com

THE FRIENDLY HOUR
© Copyright 2011 by Tom Jacobson

All rights reserved. This work is fully protected under the copyright laws of the United States of America. No part of this publication may be photocopied, reproduced, stored in a retrieval system, or transmitted, in any form or by any means, electronic, mechanical, recording, or otherwise, without the prior permission of the publisher. Additional copies of this play are available from the publisher.

Written permission is required for live performance of any sort. This includes readings, cuttings, scenes, and excerpts. For amateur and stock performances, please contact Broadway Play Publishing Inc. For all other rights contact the author c/o Playwrights Ink, 3425 W 1st St, Los Angeles, CA 90004, 213 385-4562, tom.jacobson@sbcglobal.net.

First printing: July 2011
Second printing: June 2014
I S B N: 978-0-88145-499-4

Book design: Marie Donovan
Page make-up: Adobe Indesign
Typeface: Palatino
Printed and bound in the U S A

ABOUT THE AUTHOR

Tom Jacobson has had more than 70 productions of his plays in Los Angeles and around the country, including SPERM at Circle X Theater Company, THE ORANGE GROVE at Playwrights' Arena, and the award-winning BUNBURY, TAINTED BLOOD and OUROBOROS at The Road Theater Company (all three of which are published by Broadway Play Publishing Inc). He has been a co-literary manager of The Theater @ Boston Court, a founding member of Playwrights Ink, and a board member of Cornerstone Theater Company. He teaches playwriting and related courses for U C L A Extension. His most recent productions were THE FRIENDLY HOUR at The Road Theater Company (L A Weekly Award for Best Ensemble), THE TWENTIETH-CENTURY WAY at The Theater @ Boston Court and the New York International Fringe Festival (five Ovation Award nominations, four Los Angeles Drama Critics' Circle nominations, one GLAAD Award nomination, Fringe Festival Award for Outstanding Production of a Play), and MAKING PARADISE: THE WEST HOLLYWOOD MUSICAL for Cornerstone (Critic's Choice in Back Stage West). Upcoming productions include the world premieres of THE CHINESE MASSACRE (Annotated) at Circle X and HOUSE OF THE RISING SON at Ensemble Studio Theater-L A.

THE FRIENDLY HOUR had its world premiere on 12 September 2008 by The Road Theater Company (Executive Producer, Taylor Gilbert; Producers, Aaron Kopp and Albie Selznick) in Los Angles. The cast and creative contributors were:

OPAL .... Deana Barone
WAVA .... Mara Marini
EFFIE .... Kate Mines
DORCAS .... Ann Noble
ISABELLE, LUCILLE, IRENE, EDNA, ALICE,
BARB, HAZEL, ELVERA .... Bettina Zacar
Understudies .... Shana Gagnon, Kelly Godfrey,
Lenne Klingeman, Jamie Reichner

Director .... Mark Bringelson
Assistant director .... Michael Beahm
Stage manager .... Maurie Gonzalez
Set design .... Desma Murphy
Lighting design .... Derrick McDaniel
Sound design .... Chris Moscatiello
Costume design .... Lisa Burke
Prop design .... Sarah Moretz
Dialect coach .... Linda De Vries
Graphic design .... Ammar Mahmoud

CHARACTERS

five actors:

DORCAS BRIGGLE, *a farm wife, Swedish descent, ages 21 to 94*

WAVA JAMTGAARD, DORCAS's *unmarried sister, ages 23 to 81*

EFFIE VOSS, *a farm wife, Norwegian descent, ages 22 to 95*

OPAL ZWEIFEL, *a farm wife and beautician, German descent, ages 24 to 77*

ISABELLE HAGEN, *a farm wife, recent Swedish immigrant, ages 24 to 90, also plays:*

LUCILLE OSTENSEN, OPAL's *cousin, ages 26 to 57*

IRENE DESPLINTER, *a horsewoman from Montana, ages 30 to 65*

EDNA PATTON, *a Home Services Advisor from Oklahoma, 32*

ELVERA NORMAN, *collects things, ages 56 to 67*

ALICE BJERS, ELVERA's *cousin, 65*

BARB NORLING, *a librarian, 28*

HAZEL LARSON, *a quilter and adventurous cook, 75*

Character note: All roles should be played by actresses close to the ages of the characters at the beginning of the play. Ageing should be indicated through acting, costume and possibly hairstyle, but not through make-up.

Dialogue note: As much as possible, dialogue should overlap in many of the group scens, cacophony over clarity

SETTING

The action takes place in various locations near Beresford, South Dakota, from 1934 to 2007, including several parlors, a bedroom, a porch, a library, a nursing home, and a field.

The set should be defined primarily through lighting, with a minimum of furniture, an upright piano and one closet door. Plants accumulate throughout the play.

Dedicated to the memory of Elvera Kinkner (1913-2009) with deepest gratitude to her daughter, Caryl Crozier, who gave me the archive of The Friendly Hour Club.

ACT ONE

(A popular tune from 1934 plays on the radio in the darkness. As it ends:)

DORCAS: And you can take the minutes.

WAVA: I couldn't possibly!

DORCAS: Wava!

WAVA: Dorcas, I can't!

DORCAS: Fine, I'll do it myself.

(Lights up on DORCAS BRIGGLE, *an attractive farm wife, 21. She is dressed simply and inexpensively.)*

DORCAS: *(Out)* Our new club met for the first time October 2, 1934 at the home of—

(Lights up on OPAL ZWEIFEL, *24, a farm wife dressed a little more extravagantly than* DORCAS.*)*

OPAL: *(Beaming, out)* Opal Zweifel.

DORCAS: *(Out)* With five members present:

(Lights up on EFFIE VOSS [22)] WAVA JAMTGAARD [23], *and* ISABELLE HAGEN [24], *all farm women.* EFFIE *is quite pregnant.* ISABELLE *is blonde and wears a pearl necklace.)*

EFFIE: *(Slight Norwegian accent, out)* Effie Voss.

ISABELLE: *(Strong Swedish accent, out)* Isabelle Hagen.

DORCAS: *(Out)* Dorcas Briggle.

OPAL: *(Beaming, out)* Opal Zweifel.

DORCAS: And—

(They all look at WAVA, *whose nose and cheeks are unnaturally red, maybe even a little swollen.)*

WAVA: *(Shyly, out)* Wava Jamtgaard.

ISABELLE: *Varfor behover vi en klubb?* [Why do we need a club?]

OPAL: What did she say?

DORCAS: I'm bored, Isabelle! Aren't you bored? I'm bored to death!

WAVA: *(Overlapping* DORCAS, *to* OPAL*)* She wants to know why we need a club.

DORCAS: All we do is work—swatting grain, shocking grain, kitchen work—

EFFIE: There are plenty of clubs: Ladies Aid at Nazareth Lutheran—

OPAL: The ladies club at Brooklyn Evangelical Free Church—

WAVA: At Gothland Church—

(OPAL disappears.)

DORCAS: Those are church clubs. All at different churches. We need something for all of us, more—

EFFIE: Ecumenical.

DORCAS: Ecumenical?

OPAL: *(Reappearing with coffee cups and a pot.)* What's that?

EFFIE: Not Lutheran, not Congregational, not Catholic—

(Everyone takes coffee.)

OPAL: Certainly not Catholic—!

DORCAS: Yeah, ecumenical.

EFFIE: And we don't want to be like the Progress Study Club—

WAVA: There's Just Us Girls—

DORCAS: That's an old lady club! The boringest club in South Dakota!

EFFIE: My mother's in that.

OPAL: All they do is visit and do fancywork, don'tcha know.

ISABELLE: *(Haltingly)* For a club—very— *(Gestures, frustrated.) Jag ar for upptagen for att vara med i en klubb.* [I'm too busy for a club]

WAVA: Isabelle says she's too busy—

ISABELLE: *Laga mat, ta hand om klader—* [Making dinner, making clothes—]

DORCAS: Too busy for fun? We need some fun!

WAVA: And a beautiful dress that is, Isabelle—

EFFIE: We have dances, Walter and I play—

WAVA: Like prairie flowers in May—

ISABELLE: *Tack sa mycket.* [Thanks so much.]

DORCAS: The dances are wonderful, Effie. Walter's fiddle makes it so lively—

WAVA: Oh, yes! I wish I could dance, but listening is nice—

OPAL: Palmer and I love to dance!

DORCAS: But how many times have you got all dressed up and excited to go and your husband gets peeved and decides he wants to just stay home—

(The others just look at each other.)

DORCAS: Maybe that's just Clarence, then—

EFFIE: Really, Dorcas, you should get out more, for your own good.

DORCAS: But I want my fun. Our fun. Remember, Effie, in school when we used to do stunts, and sing those crazy songs—

EFFIE: That time we all ditched school and the School Board came out—

DORCAS & EFFIE: And chased us around the park—!

WAVA: And Arnie Stordal caught that sunfish and ran around with it—

OPAL & WAVA: In his hand all day!

EFFIE: That was a time!

WAVA: We picked lilac and wild pasque flowers—

DORCAS: But it's not like that any more is it, girls?

WAVA: Nobody has any money.

EFFIE: We're all married— *(To* WAVA*)* I mean, most of us—

DORCAS: I'm not ready to be an old lady yet!

OPAL: We *have* to work! With the drought and the dust—I'm operating the linotype at the Beresford Republic just to make ends meet.

EFFIE: Our families need us— *(To* WAVA*)* Your parents need you, your brother needs you—

DORCAS: With nothing but work, I could go crazy and become a menace to society!

WAVA: And the wind moaning all the time!

OPAL: Too late!

EFFIE: It would be nice to have a grown-up conversation once in a while.

WAVA: But what would our club do?

DORCAS: Well, fun things. Like—like—Happy Birthday, Wava!

WAVA: Oh, Dorcas!

DORCAS: My big sister is turning twenty-three next week!

EFFIE: Happy Birthday, Wava!

ISABELLE: *Gratulationer pa fodelsedagen.* [Happy Birthday!]

OPAL: Twenty-three! I can't believe it!

DORCAS: We can celebrate birthdays, anniversaries—

OPAL: *(Patting EFFIE's belly)* Babies—

WAVA: We could do crafts!

ISABELLE: *(Modeling her outfit) Dela monster!* [Share patterns!]

WAVA: *Det dar ar verlkligen fint, Isabelle!* [That really is nice, Isabelle!]

OPAL: I made a nice lunch, by the way—

EFFIE: But isn't that a little...selfish? Isn't it our Christian duty to think of others? Maybe we could do works of charity, make donations—

OPAL: Covered dishes for old people!

DORCAS: Effie, nobody has a penny to spare—last spring I had to pick wild asparagus out by the train tracks—

WAVA: Maybe a little, though. Just ten cents—

OPAL: We could have dues. Every—month—would we meet every month?

EFFIE: And we could vote—

OPAL: Yes, vote!

EFFIE: —On what to do with it.

DORCAS: What a wonderful idea, Effie!

WAVA: Mercy! It sounds so serious!

EFFIE: *(Taking out a coin)* Here's a dime!

OPAL: *(Taking out another)* Here's mine! *(Taking out a cheap coin purse)* And I'll donate this coin purse for our treasury. Palmer got it from the bank, but I'm sure he won't mind.

ISABELLE: *(Proffering a coin) Om det bara ar tio cent.* [If it's only a dime.]

DORCAS: I don't know if I've got it right now—

(OPAL collects the coins in the purse.)

WAVA: *(Digging in her purse)* Never mind, Dorcas, I'll do yours and mine.

EFFIE: How about the first Tuesday of every month? Two in the P M?

WAVA: That sounds nice.

DORCAS: I can do that.

ISABELLE: *Jag maste ga tidigt.* [I might have to leave early.]

OPAL: Something to look forward to, dontcha know!

WAVA: I'm sure that's fine if you have to leave early, Isabelle.

EFFIE: What about officers?

DORCAS: Officers?

EFFIE: A President, Secretary—we'll need a Treasurer—

DORCAS: I think you should be President, Effie.

EFFIE: Me? It was your idea.

DORCAS: But you're so organized. Everyone for Effie?

(All raise hands.)

EFFIE: Heavens! Well, all right.

DORCAS: Our first President of the—what shall we call ourselves—? The Go-Pher-Fun Club?

EFFIE: Oh, no, that's a terrible name! We're not vermin! *(She makes a gopher face.)*

DORCAS: Then what?

OPAL: The Lunch Club?

EFFIE: No.

OPAL: The Beresford Club?

DORCAS: That sounds a little grand, doesn't it? None of us live in town.

OPAL: Farm Friends?

EFFIE: Ishda! How about The Friendly Hour? A time every month when we do—

WAVA: Friendly things!

EFFIE: For us and for our neighbors.

DORCAS: Oh, I like that. Shall we vote—oh! Madame President?

EFFIE: All those in favor of The Friendly Hour signify by saying "aye".

ALL: Aye!

EFFIE: Motion carries. Even though it wasn't a formal motion, but we'll get there.

OPAL: *(Standing to go in the kitchen)* Could anyone eat a little lunch?

EFFIE: Opal, such a good hostess.

DORCAS: I'm starving.

ISABELLE: *Ja tack.* [Yes, please!]

OPAL: I have rolls, chicken, potato soup, fruit salad, pickles—

WAVA: Your famous crisp, green pickles!

OPAL: And date cake! A new recipe, so you can tell me if it's all right. *(She heads off to the kitchen.)*

ISABELLE: *(Following* OPAL*) Lat mig hjalpa!* [Let me help!]

WAVA: Dorcas, I'm so excited. Mercy!

EFFIE: How's Clarence?

DORCAS: Oh, fine. Still peeved at my father 'cause he didn't come to the wedding.

WAVA: There was *dancing* at the wedding!

DORCAS: Dancing is immoral, Pa says.

EFFIE: Depends on the dancing, I spose.

DORCAS: Walter all right?

EFFIE: Wore out from getting what's left of the corn in. He says hello, Wava.

WAVA: Oh, that's nice.

*(*EFFIE, DORCAS *and* WAVA *sip their coffee. Lights up on* ISABELLE *and* OPAL *in the kitchen cutting up pickles to serve.)*

OPAL: *(Confidentially)* Like I say, Dorcas is frosted that Effie's run off with her idea. That's why she suggested Effie for President—her sideways way of getting back at her, dontcha know. They used to be best friends until Effie went away to college—I don't understand it. Well, never mind, it's none of my business.

WAVA: *(Overlapping* OPAL*)* Dorcas, I found this pattern for the cutest little Christmas ornaments made from medicine bottles—angels and such—

EFFIE: Medicine bottles—?

OPAL: Wava and Dorcas got a lot of worries.

WAVA: Could we share crafts like that in the Club?

OPAL: With Wava taking care of her folks and her brother—

DORCAS: Ask the President.

OPAL: And their father's got something wrong with him.

EFFIE: I was thinking we could have contests—fun, like you said. I brought that bridal shower game with the flower names—

OPAL: In his head, dontcha know. That time he got mad at Marvin and hung him upside-down in the cistern for a whole day.

DORCAS: I was hoping we could sometimes talk about books we've read.

OPAL: He never was right after that.

(Lights out on ISABELLE *and* OPAL.*)*

EFFIE: Now *that* sounds like an old lady club. Books!

DORCAS: Effie, you're the smartest girl I know—you got to read all them books in college. The rest of us didn't have opportunity for such.

EFFIE: All *those* books.

DORCAS: See? I *need* to read more books!

EFFIE: I didn't read so much. I studied dramatics!

WAVA: Dorcas, you're a runner not a reader. And a climber!

EFFIE: *Uffda!* I thought you were gonna break your neck scrambling up the Buffalo Jump. I almost fainted!

DORCAS: You always were a big chicken—woulda left my bones there to rot with the rest of 'em.

EFFIE: That was a time.

DORCAS: Listen to us. Married and dead.

WAVA: Least I'm safe.

*(*OPAL *comes in carrying a couple of lit kerosene lamps, and* ISABELLE *bears plates of pickles.)*

OPAL: Getting dark so early already!

ISABELLE: *(Handing out pickle plates.) Varsagod. Varsagod. Varsagod.* [Please. Please. Please.]

DORCAS & WAVA: *Tack sa mycket.* [Thanks so much.]

EFFIE: Thanks, Isabelle.

OPAL: What'd we miss?

DORCAS: Silly memories of the Buffalo Jump.

OPAL: Hasn't changed, don'tcha know. I should have Palmer go down there and clean that mess up.

EFFIE: If the Indians didn't see fit to clean up after themselves, why should we?

ISABELLE: *(Getting her coat) Jag ar sa ledsen att behova ga.* [I'm so sorry I have to leave.]

OPAL: Already? We haven't eaten!

WAVA: *Isabelle, jag ar sa ledsen ocksa!* [Isabelle, I'm sorry, too!]

ISABELLE: *Jag maste laga kvallsmat-supe at Ragnar.* [I have to make supper for Ragnar.]

EFFIE: We haven't even played our game!

WAVA: She needs to make supper for Ragnar.

DORCAS: A game?

ISABELLE: *Hejda!* [Good-bye!]

DORCAS & WAVA: *Hejda,* Isabelle!

OPAL: *(Miming telephone)* Do you want to use my telephone to call Ragnar to get you?

ISABELLE: *Nej, jag vill ga, det ar stangt.* [No, I will walk. It's close.]

EFFIE: Opal, not everybody has a telephone.

ISABELLE: *Hejda! (She leaves.)*

DORCAS: It's too early to start supper.

OPAL: I think Ragnar wants a little something before supper.

(They all giggle.)

EFFIE: Now, girls, let's not have that kind of talk. *(Produces some papers and pencils)* I brought a game.

WAVA: A game! Will there be prizes?

OPAL: Jelly beans?

DORCAS: I will never play croquet with you again.

OPAL: *(Reading)* Wedding Bouquet?

EFFIE: You have to answer each question with a flower. The first one is "What the groom did when he mustered up his courage."

(They all look blank.)

EFFIE: Oh, come on! A common flower.

(Still blank looks)

EFFIE: Aster!

WAVA: Aster? I don't get it.

DORCAS: Aster—he asked her!

OPAL: Ohh! That's cute!

EFFIE: What time he did it?

DORCAS: Morning glory...?

EFFIE: No...

OPAL: Four o'clock!

EFFIE: See? It's simple!

DORCAS: *(Out)* Effie Voss had charge of the entertainment.

EFFIE: What pouted till he did?

OPAL: Two lips!

WAVA: *(Out)* Which everyone enjoyed.

EFFIE: What ferocious beast kept uninvited guests away from the church entrance?

WAVA: Tiger lily?

DORCAS: *(Out)* And a tasty lunch was served—

OPAL: *(Out, beaming)* By hostess Opal Zweifel.

EFFIE: Who gave the bride away?

OPAL & WAVA: Poppy!

(Lighting change as DORCAS, EFFIE, OPAL, *and* WAVA *continue the game but also change their clothes.* ISABELLE *appears as well, also changing her clothes.)*

EFFIE: Who performed the ceremony?

DORCAS: *(With little enthusiasm)* Jack in the pulpit.

EFFIE: What was the bride's dress trimmed in?

DORCAS & OPAL: Queen Anne's lace.

EFFIE: Who were the bridesmaids?

OPAL: Rose!

WAVA: Violet!

DORCAS: Daisy.

EFFIE: Who tried to vamp the groom?

OPAL & WAVA: Black-eyed susan!

(When she changes clothes, DORCAS *becomes pregnant.* EFFIE *is pregnant again.)*

EFFIE: What did the best man give them for a household pet?

DORCAS, OPAL, & WAVA: Dandy lion!

*(*EFFIE, ISABELLE, *and* OPAL *leave.)*

DORCAS: *(Out)* November 1, 1938.

WAVA: *(Out)* Our Friendly Hour Club met at the home of hostess Dorcas Briggle.

(Dorcas and Wava sniff the air.)

Dorcas: I think it's gone.

Wava: I can't smell it.

Dorcas: Maybe we're just used to it.

Wava: No, it's gone. I'm sure of it.

Dorcas: *(Out)* Roll call: What did you think of our book selection? Opal Zweifel?

Opal: *(Appearing)* It was too long! *(Sniffs suspiciously.)*

Dorcas: But it's a best-seller! Wava Jamtgaard?

Wava: I tried to read it, but I couldn't possibly finish it in time.

Dorcas: Effie Voss?

Effie: *(Appearing)* Boring! *(Sniffs suspiciously)*

Dorcas: It won the Pulitzer Prize! Isabelle Hagen?

Isabelle: *(Appearing, carrying a sleeping baby)* My English is not so good yet. *(Sniffs suspiciously)*

Dorcas: Dorcas Briggle? I liked it very much. Prissy was so funny and I cried when Atlanta burned. I've decided nothing's more fun than going to bed with a book, curling up by the light, and letting it take you somewhere you've never been. When I know I have some time to read, I get so excited I can hardly breathe.

(Everyone sniffs. Dorcas looks at Wava in a panic.)

Effie: Dorcas, was there a—?

Opal: Worse than Palmer's cigars!

Isabelle: Skunk! I smell skunk!

Wava: Must be across the pasture—

Effie: I think it's in the house.

Opal: In the house?! *(Gets up)*

Dorcas: No, no, it's dead!

EFFIE: You have a dead skunk in your house?

DORCAS: No, it's me.

(They sniff her and recoil.)

DORCAS: Clarence and I skinned a skunk last week and we can't make it go away. He stinks, too.

OPAL: Oh, I know how it is. Palmer's smoke just clings!

EFFIE: Why'd you skin a skunk?

WAVA: There's a government bounty!

EFFIE: How much for skunk?

DORCAS: The hardest twenty-five cents I ever earned.

EFFIE: Well, at least you'll be able to pay dues this month.

(ISABELLE's baby starts to cry.)

OPAL: *(Out, holding coin purse.)* Treasurer's report: old balance—six dollars and thirty cents. Dues:

(They each put a dime in the coin purse. WAVA reaches for the baby, and ISABELLE gives it to her.)

OPAL: *(Out)* Fifty cents. New balance: six dollars and eighty cents.

DORCAS: I'm sorry none of you liked the book.

EFFIE: Dorcas, it's fine to read whatever you want for your own good—it broadens your horizons, I'm sure. But for Club I think we should steer clear of religion and politics.

(The baby stops crying.)

DORCAS: Politics?

EFFIE: Heavens! What could be more political than a war book?

DORCAS: But that war was almost sixty-five years ago.

EFFIE: Even so, it's just not polite. Besides, why should we talk about politics when we all agree? We're all the same. That's what's nice about our club.

DORCAS: I'm not so sure we're all—

WAVA: Doesn't somebody have a birthday coming up?

(WAVA *gives the baby back to* ISABELLE.)

OPAL: That's right! Effie, which one is it, if I may ask?

EFFIE: As if you didn't know, Opal, you're terrible. I'm going to be twenty-seven next week and I'm not afraid to admit it.

OPAL: I can give you a nice finger wave to celebrate, don'tcha know!

DORCAS: Well, happy birthday, Effie. I see Walter gave you another present.

EFFIE: Oh, you're worse than Opal. And Clarence finally gave you one as well.

DORCAS: Not like we haven't been trying!

WAVA: (*Touching* DORCAS' *belly*) I want a girl! Dress her old-fashioned in gingham—

EFFIE: Dorcas, you're awful!

DORCAS: Oh, I hope not! I got no patience for lace and dollies. All I can think is Ma telling me never to have children 'cause they're too much worry.

WAVA: Isabelle, did you sew that elegant dress?

ISABELLE: *Ja.*

OPAL: What a pretty print!

ISABELLE: *Tack sa mycket.*

WAVA: Simplicity?

EFFIE: Butterick?

ISABELLE: Me! I make myself. And now I go!

WAVA: You just got here!

ISABELLE: I know, but Ragnar—

EFFIE: Isabelle, for four years you've left early!

ISABELLE: *(Putting on her coat)* No choice, I am afraid. *Hejda!*

ALL: *Hejda!* Good-bye.

(ISABELLE leaves.)

OPAL: Ragnar.

(They all shake their heads, smiling knowingly.)

OPAL: Oh, Effie, Walter left this at the American Legion dance. *(Pulls out a violin case)* I found it when we were cleaning up and thought he might need it.

(OPAL passes the case to DORCAS, who passes it to WAVA.)

EFFIE: Thank heavens, Opal! Walter accused me of hiding it.

WAVA: *(Stroking the case)* It's beautiful.

EFFIE: He's been tearing up the house, even the barn! Just lost without it.

(EFFIE takes the case from WAVA, who parts with it somewhat reluctantly.)

EFFIE: Wava, did you wanna borrow that?

WAVA: No, no! I only play piano.

DORCAS: Did I tell you Clarence and I got an A S C S subsidy?

EFFIE: I don't believe in government charity.

OPAL: What for, Dorcas?

WAVA: Oh, it's wonderful! To drain the slough—

DORCAS: *(Pointing)* In the south meadow. Also to pick the rocks and cut down those ugly little willows and chinese elms.

DORCAS: Plough under those weeds and get some use out of it.

EFFIE: Nothing worse than wasted land.

OPAL: Are you hiring?

WAVA: Wolves hide in those trees!

DORCAS: Oh, no, we need the money, so we're doing it ourselves.

EFFIE: Haven't been wolves in fifty years!

OPAL: Oh, you poor thing—picking rocks!

WAVA: It's a lot of work!

DORCAS: I don't mind—gotta be done!

WAVA: Marvin's gonna miss that slough.

EFFIE: Walter, too. Best duck slough in Union County.

OPAL: Good pheasant land, too, dontcha know.

DORCAS: Clarence'd rather have the money than the ducks. *(She quacks like a duck, rather well.)*

WAVA: Oh, Dorcas!

OPAL: Don't let Palmer hear you, he'd take you along as a decoy!

EFFIE: I wouldn't mind—I like hunting! *(She mimes aiming, makes a meadowlark call, and "shoots" rather expertly.)*

WAVA: Oh, but you don't shoot meadowlarks?

EFFIE: No, it's just the only birdcall I know.

(OPAL caws like a crow.)

DORCAS: Wava, do your loon!

WAVA: Dorcas, I couldn't possibly!

EFFIE: Oh, do it, Wava. Don't be such a chicken!

(OPAL does the crow call again.)

WAVA: You're all terrible—making me do things I'd never— *(She wails like a loon.)*

EFFIE: Oh! Sends chills up my spine, that sound.

(WAVA wails again. OPAL caws. DORCAS quacks, and finally EFFIE does the meadowlark call. They repeat a few times, not hearing a knock at the door. Suddenly, as their calls continue, LUCILLE bursts into the room in a gust of wind and snowflakes wearing winter clothing and carrying a small planter with blooming paperwhites. She has red hair, and there is snow on her shoulders. She stands there, smiling, looking confused. After a moment, they notice her and the birdcalls cease.)

OPAL: *(Jumping up)* Oh! Everyone, you know my cousin, Lucille Ostensen.

WAVA: Oh, dear, is it snowing hard?

OPAL: We voted last month to invite her to The Friendly Hour. Lucille, do you know any birdcalls?

EFFIE: Opal, it's not mandatory—

OPAL: Of course not—just for fun—Lucille is so fun— you'll see—

DORCAS: Welcome to The Friendly Hour, Lucille! You need some coffee.

WAVA: Are those daffodils? It's winter!

EFFIE: Let me get your coat, Lucille!

(They start to crowd around her but step back when LUCILLE suddenly makes the strange, gulping call of the American bittern.)

OPAL: Lucille!

EFFIE: *Uffda!*

(They stare at LUCILLE for a moment as she repeats the sound.)

DORCAS: It's a sloughpumper!

EFFIE: A what?

DORCAS: You know, a bittern!

WAVA: A sloughpumper!

(EFFIE takes LUCILLE's coat, WAVA takes the paperwhites, DORCAS gets LUCILLE a cup of coffee, and OPAL leads LUCILLE to a chair. WAVA sets the paperwhites where everyone can see.)

WAVA: The hidden talents!

OPAL: I just knew you'd fit right in!

WAVA: You must have forced them! So delicate!

OPAL: Lucille is so good with flowers—her whole house, all winter, even. What are those, Lucille—?

EFFIE: They're narcissus bulbs.

OPAL: A green thumb, two of them, well, she's practically green all over, don'tcha know.

(OPAL catches her breath as LUCILLE sniffs the air, looks puzzled, then turns to DORCAS.)

WAVA: And don't these smell lovely, too!

OPAL: And not just houseplants! Her garden starts early in the spring, crocuses and such, all manner of bulbs, straight through till fall, all planned out so there's always color. The biggest dahlias you've ever seen, like dinner plates, and she picks off the begonia blossoms so the ones that remain get huge, absolutely huge, don't you, Lucille?

(LUCILLE smiles, is perhaps about to speak, when OPAL launches in again.)

OPAL: Lucille's married to August Ostensen and they just moved to his parents' farm east of town—

EFFIE: *(Going to the window)* Lucille, is that your Ford in the ditch?

(All but LUCILLE *rush to the window.)*

OPAL: Why it's a blizzard!

WAVA: Mercy!

DORCAS: It's early for a storm like this.

EFFIE: We should have cancelled.
Dorcas, do you have blankets? We might have to stay
over.

WAVA: I can hardly see a thing!

DORCAS: *(Out)* It stormed, so our meeting turned into—

WAVA: *(Out)* A sleepover!

*(*DORCAS *gets blankets and starts passing them out.* EFFIE
brings out kerosene lamps. WAVA *lights candles. Sound of
howling wind.* LUCILLE *tidies up the room in some way,
with slightly compulsive energy.)*

DORCAS & EFFIE: *(Out)* We slept on the parlor floor.

OPAL: *(On the telephone)* I know, Palmer, but it's
impossible—

WAVA: Aren't candles wonderful? So old-fashioned
and romantic!

OPAL: *(On the telephone)* I'm sorry you had to do the
milking by yourself—

EFFIE: Looks like another long winter.

OPAL: *(On the telephone)* Eat your favorite—

DORCAS: *(Bringing a chamber pot)* I can't even see the
outhouse, so I guess we'll need to use this.

OPAL: *(On the phone and gesturing for the chamber pot)* —
Popcorn dumped in milk!

*(*DORCAS *hands* OPAL *the chamber pot.* OPAL *clutches it.)*

OPAL: *(On the telephone)* I really am with the girls!
Dorcas, you talk to him.

EFFIE: Remember last year the snow was so deep—

WAVA: It was terrible!

DORCAS: *(On the phone)* Hello, Palmer?

EFFIE: We were stuck home for two weeks till the snowplow came!

OPAL: Didn't thaw until June!

DORCAS: *(Gesturing to the other room for* OPAL*)* We're right here at my house.

EFFIE: That's when the kids found Tessie tied to a tree with a bullet in her head. I gave Walter a piece of my mind about that! The ground was frozen, he said.

OPAL: She was the egg-eater?

EFFIE: Long as I live, I'm never letting him get another dog.

*(*OPAL *takes the chamber pot and goes to the other room.)*

DORCAS: Hush, Palmer. I won't have talk like that in my house.

WAVA: Mercy! That just doesn't sound like him.

EFFIE: And I love dogs more than anything. But that's it.

DORCAS: Well, *I'm* in my house!

*(*DORCAS *hangs up angrily, slightly shaken. She sees them all looking at her.)*

DORCAS: Let's have a dance! Who wants to?

WAVA: A dance? I couldn't possibly!

EFFIE: We shouldn't dance if we're expecting.

WAVA: How about Table Up?

DORCAS: We play that all the time.

EFFIE: That's occult!

DORCAS: *(Energetically moving furniture)* I danced on Saturday and I'm no worse for wear. My teats aren't as big as yours so they don't get in the way.

(WAVA and LUCILLE each put two fingers under the table and try to lift it.)

WAVA: Dorcas, mercy! What's got into you!

EFFIE: Dorcas Briggle, you are beyond the pale!

WAVA: Table up, table up, table up, table up, table up, table up, table up, table up—!

EFFIE: Your silhouette was in style when we were in high school, but as a mother—

DORCAS: *(Handing EFFIE sheet music)* Oh, hush up about my silhouette and play! *(Holding out her hand)* Wava?

(EFFIE sits down at the piano.)

WAVA: Dorcas, no! I don't know how.

DORCAS: Then we'll have lessons. Clarence taught me and I got two left feet! Lucille? Stop that! Is my house dirty?

(LUCILLE stops her compulsive cleaning and takes DORCAS's hand.)

DORCAS: Maestro, if you please?

(EFFIE plays a peppy big band dance tune. DORCAS leads LUCILLE in a swing dance. There is only slight awkwardness at the beginning, then they start to have fun.)

DORCAS: *(Instructing as they go)* First you do this—then this—relax, Lucille!

WAVA: Lucille, you're a natural!

DORCAS: That's it! That's it! Lucille, you're better than any smelly old man!

OPAL: *(Coming out with the chamber pot)* Palmer give you a hard time?

DORCAS: No, Opal, you're staying the night thanks to an Act of God and Palmer doesn't have a choice. Put down that pot and dance!

OPAL: *(Grabbing* WAVA *as a dance partner)* I love this club!

EFFIE: Not right for girls to dance together.

WAVA: Opal, no, stop! I couldn't possibly!

(All four of them dance enthusiastically as EFFIE *plays.)*

DORCAS: *(Out)* Hostess Dorcas Briggle had the entertainment—

OPAL: *(Out)* And taught us a lively dance.

EFFIE: I do not approve. I do not! *(But she doesn't stop playing.)*

WAVA: *(Out)* We hardly slept a wink we had such fun.

EFFIE: Jumping around like colored people—or wild Indians!

OPAL: *(Out)* The husbands were a little peeved.

*(*EFFIE *gets up from the piano, but the music continues and the others keep dancing.)*

EFFIE: *(Out)* For the business portion of our meeting—

(Two by two, the others stop dancing and start changing clothes. LUCILLE *leaves.)*

OPAL: *(Out)* We voted to give—

ALL: *(Out)* —One dollar—

(While changing clothes, OPAL *briefly rolls a rolling pin over her thighs to rid herself of cellulite.)*

EFFIE: *(Out)* —To Laura Branmoe's family—

DORCAS & OPAL: *(Out)* As their house burnt down.

EFFIE: *(Out)* Plans were made for our Christmas meeting—

WAVA: *(Out)* With Secret Pals gifts of—

ALL: *(Out)* —One dollar—

OPAL: *(Out)* And holiday treats brought by each.

EFFIE: *(Out)* There being no further business old or new, the meeting was adjourned.

(In changing clothes, DORCAS is briefly topless and examines her breasts in a mirror, finding them wanting.)

OPAL & WAVA: *(Out)* A tasty lunch was served—

(Lights out on everyone but DORCAS)

DORCAS: *(Gazing in the mirror, topless and pensive, out)* By hostess Dorcas Briggle.

(Lights out on DORCAS and up dimly on WAVA in bed. She is wide awake, frozen in fear and staring at a bundled-up MAN in a mask standing at the foot of her bed. They stare at each other for a moment. The MAN takes a step toward WAVA. She looks frightened, then excited, then frightened again. They stare another moment.)

WAVA: *(Barely able to speak)* What do you want?

(No answer)

WAVA: Who are you?

MAN: *(In a strange, disguised voice)* Guess!

WAVA: I couldn't possibly!

MAN: You must!

WAVA: Is it...Walter?

MAN: Noooo!

(The MAN throws a small straw goat at WAVA and she catches it.)

WAVA: *(No longer scared)* A goat! The Julebukk! You're Julebukking! I know who you are! It's Palmer! Palmer loves Julebukking!

VOICES: Noooo!

WAVA: Mercy! Who else is here?!

(Three other strangely dressed MEN *run into the room carrying kerosene lamps. One of them has a big belly.)*

MEN: Guess!

WAVA: I'm calling Marvin! It's too early for Julebukking! *(Calls)* Marvin!

MAN TWO: We've taken care of your brother.

MAN THREE: He can't help you now!

MAN FOUR: You must do our bidding!

MEN ONE & TWO: Give us beer!

MAN THREE: *(In a much more feminine voice)* No beer! I thought we said no beer!

WAVA: Effie! *(Delighted)* Effie, that's you!

DORCAS & OPAL: Effie!

WAVA: You gave it away! *(Pointing to the others)* Dorcas? Opal?

*(*DORCAS, EFFIE, *and* OPAL *take off their disguises.* EFFIE, *pregnant again, is the fat one.)*

WAVA: *(Pointing to the first* MAN*)* Lucille?

*(*MAN *shakes his head.)*

WAVA: Isabelle!

*(*ISABELLE *takes off her disguise.)*

ISABELLE: Now you must to come with us!

EFFIE: We're going to Lucille's next!

WAVA: What time is it?

DORCAS: Two?

OPAL: Three?

EFFIE: We tried Saugstad's, but their door was locked!

WAVA: I don't have a costume!

DORCAS: *(Producing a bundle)* Marvin gave me some cast-offs.

(They start dressing WAVA *in men's clothing.)*

WAVA: Where are the men?

EFFIE: They went their own way—

DORCAS: To town! Palmer wanted to scare all of Beresford.

OPAL: *(Gestures)* Drinking.

DORCAS: Effie couldn't condone it.

EFFIE: There are just other ways to have fun.

WAVA: *(Now disguised, and using her disguised voice)* Then let's go have it!

(They all run off except for EFFIE, *who starts the minutes as she changes to "Christmasy" clothes [but she is still pregnant]:)*

EFFIE: *(Out)* December 4, 1945. The Friendly Hour Club met at the home of Wava Jamtgaard for our Christmas party. *(She produces a tiny Christmas gift.)* Six members were present for the roll call topic of "worst chore"—

DORCAS: *(Appearing as she changes to "Christmasy" clothes, with a gift)* Oh, no, let's tell "dreams now that the war is over."

EFFIE: *(Irritated, but persevering)* Wava Jamtgaard?

WAVA: *(Appearing as she changes, with a gift)* My dream is that electricity will come to everybody's farm by next year.

EFFIE: Isabelle Hagen?

ISABELLE: *(Appears, changing, with a gift)* Dat I will have de electric sewing machine! *(Posing)* You need help in kitchen? Before I leave, ja?

WAVA: Oh, no, Isabelle—

(But ISABELLE *has disappeared.)*

EFFIE: Dorcas Briggle?

WAVA: I best go help Isabelle! It's my kitchen!
(Disappears)

DORCAS: My dream is for The Friendly Hour to meet
every month again now that gas rationing is done.

EFFIE: Opal Zweifel?

OPAL: *(Appearing, changing, with a gift)* A reliable cure
for constipation.

EFFIE: Opal, there's no call for—

DORCAS: Rhubarb!

ISABELLE: *(Calling from the kitchen)* Mineral oil!

WAVA: *(Sticks her head in from the kitchen)* Coffee?

OPAL: That doesn't work for me—

WAVA: Does anyone want coffee?

(All raise their hands. WAVA *disappears.)*

OPAL: My real dream now that the war's over is to quit
the linotype and open my own beauty parlor.

EFFIE: At least that's better than constipation.

DORCAS: You're so good at styling, Opal.

OPAL: And I like talking to folks.

DORCAS: You'd make them comfortable—

EFFIE: You'd be a shrewd businesswoman, I bet!

OPAL: Or maybe a bakery! Palmer says my desserts are
made of love.

WAVA: Nobody bakes like you.

OPAL: I think feeding people is about the nicest thing
you can do.

EFFIE: I believe it's my turn.

DORCAS: Jesus fed people.

EFFIE: Effie Voss? My dream is like Dorcas's—I want
everything to be the way it was again. *(Quickly)* And
my worst chore is laundry in winter.

OPAL: Oh, it's impossible, isn't it?

DORCAS: Frozen overalls!

EFFIE: Irene DeSplinter?

IRENE: *(Appearing, with a gift)* Chore or dream?

*(IRENE [played by same actress as ISABELLE] wears slightly
more "western" clothes, and her accent is different from the
others. She always wears a hat and a jacket, and she has an
impressive bust and dark hair.)*

EFFIE: Whichever you like.

DORCAS & OPAL: Dream!

IRENE: Mountains. This part of South Dakota needs
some mountains. How do you stand so much flatness
with no trees? My God, it just goes on and on and on!

WAVA: *(Returning with coffee for everyone)* Is Montana
mountains all over?

*(EFFIE gathers all the Christmas presents and puts them in
one place where everyone can see.)*

IRENE: And does the wind ever stop? Every time I go
out here I nearly blow away. My skin's all windburned,
you know what I'm talking about, Wava. In fact, I got
some Watkins salve you can borrow—

DORCAS: You brought some palominos with, I hear.

IRENE: But only a few, as Bob's folks got such a bitty
little farm. Three hundred acres! How the hell do you
make a living on that?

EFFIE & DORCAS: We don't, always.

(They look at each other in surprise.)

IRENE: *(Taking out cigarettes)* Mind if I smoke?

WAVA: *(Quietly overlapping)* Excuse me, I'll see if I can pry Isabelle out of my kitchen. *(Disappears)*

OPAL: *(Getting up)* Wava prefers for her brother's sake that cigarettes go on the porch. He had a touch of TB years ago.

IRENE: *(As she and OPAL go to the porch)* As long as the damn wind doesn't blow out my smoke.

DORCAS: *(When they are alone)* Effie...

EFFIE: I don't mind the hells and damns so much, but she took the Lord's name in vain. And I know it's very modern for ladies to smoke—I swear sometimes Opal reeks like she's been at Palmer's cigars—but still, Dorcas!

DORCAS: You know, Effie, I'll never forget how you took Gwenneth over to visit the Kinkners during the war so she could see Germans were just as nice as anyone else.

EFFIE: It's not the same thing.

DORCAS: At least she hasn't asked for a drink.

EFFIE: Heavens!

(DORCAS and EFFIE drink their coffee. On the porch, IRENE smokes and OPAL talks.)

OPAL: I'm sure Wava deeply appreciates your advice, but that's not windburn on her face.

IRENE: It ain't?

OPAL: She had terrible blemishes when she was eighteen, and there was this boy she liked, and she asked Doctor Hoard what she could do about it, and he burned the blemishes off which left that permanent red swollenness.

IRENE: Oh, my God, Opal! My God!

OPAL: She's terribly self-conscious about it, and I guess you know she's not married.

IRENE: I'm making a crappy impression! How'm I gonna get back in the saddle after that?

OPAL: We forget about Wava's face 'cause we seen her all our lives. Like I say, that's one of the reasons Dorcas started our club, so Wava can be around people who don't stare.

(Inside, WAVA brings EFFIE and DORCAS a plate of cookies.)

IRENE: I won't! I won't! God! Whatever happened to that boy?

OPAL: Oh, that'd be gossip, don'tcha know.

DORCAS: Christmas cookies!

EFFIE: Irene's a character, isn't she?

WAVA: Oh, I like her so much. She's lively and she means well. Do you think she'd want to be a 4-H leader?

EFFIE: Just the same, I'm wondering if we don't need some kind of—you know—*standard* for who we invite to The Friendly Hour.

DORCAS: Well, it's a little late now...

EFFIE: You know, like the Eastern Star...

IRENE: *(Coming back in with OPAL)* Oh, God, Wava, do you have any bourbon?

DORCAS: Eleanor Roosevelt!

OPAL: Mmm, Christmas cookies!

ALL: What?

DORCAS: What do you think of Eleanor Roosevelt?

EFFIE: Politics, Dorcas...!

DORCAS: It's not politics. She's not First Lady any more.

EFFIE: All the more reason she should be quiet.

OPAL: She could use some help with her hair.

DORCAS: I think she's the greatest woman alive, if not the greatest who ever lived.

EFFIE: Dorcas Briggle, you are not dragging me into an argument about that woman—

WAVA: Irene, Isabelle and I need your help in the kitchen.

IRENE: *(As she leaves with* WAVA*)* Eleanor Roosevelt has   : balls!

(As soon as IRENE *is gone,* DORCAS *and* OPAL *burst into giggles.)*

EFFIE: Not funny. *Not!*

OPAL: It's different in Montana.

EFFIE: We don't have room in The Friendly Hour for... cowhands!

OPAL: She's having a hard time, don'tcha know. Bob's ranch failed and they came back to live with his parents 'cause they have to—

DORCAS: I know that feeling.

OPAL: Bob's family is Catholic, but Irene says Bob says he doesn't believe in God.

EFFIE: *(Impulsively smacks* OPAL*)* Yes, he does!

DORCAS: He doesn't? Really?

EFFIE: Everybody believes in God.

OPAL: So they don't go to church.

EFFIE: Not even to Mass?

OPAL: *(Sotto voce)* And I think he drinks.

EFFIE: Drinking's all those Belgians know.

DORCAS: Effie, now would be a really good time to be a Christian.

WAVA: *(Bursting in with* ISABELLE*)* Everyone, it's Irene's birthday!

OPAL: Oh, my!

ISABELLE: She is in de kitchen crying.

WAVA: She said she's gone lame and it's time to shoot her.

DORCAS: Effie, what was that birthday poetry game we played a few years ago?

EFFIE: That was such a silly one!

WAVA: But you were so good at it!

OPAL: Let's do it for Irene!

ISABELLE: I will tell her. Den I go home. *(Disappears)*

EFFIE: No, Isabelle—!

OPAL: You'd think Ragnar'd be over that at his age!

DORCAS: Now we have to.

EFFIE: Dorcas Briggle! Sometimes you just frost me.

DORCAS: *(Passing out paper and pencils)* What rhymes with Irene?

EFFIE: Hush. I'm writing. And I know exactly what to say.

DORCAS: Effie—

WAVA: I can think of rhymes but not any pretty words to go with 'em.

DORCAS: You think of pretty words all the time. You should write them down.

WAVA: I'll get Irene. *(Disappears)*

EFFIE: This is easy!

*(*EFFIE *chuckles. The others look at her uneasily.)*

DORCAS: My Gwenneth writes poetry.

OPAL: And she's only eight!

DORCAS: Seven.

OPAL: Oh, my!

WAVA: *(Appearing)* Here comes the birthday girl.

(IRENE appears, cautiously.)

DORCAS: Irene, we have a birthday tradition in The Friendly Hour.

OPAL: *(Raising her hand)* Our friend Irene is pretty keen.

DORCAS: *(Raising her hand)* If you need a palomin', ask that horsey gal Irene. *(With some trepidation)* Effie?

EFFIE: Keep in mind I'm no Badger Clark—

DORCAS: Oh, I don't like Badger Clark.

OPAL: *(To IRENE)* He's a South Dakota cowboy poet.

DORCAS: He has thin lips.

EFFIE: I think that I have never seen a tree as lovely as Irene.

IRENE: That's because you live in South Dakota. I mean, thank you, that's nice.

(Everyone looks at WAVA.)

WAVA: I worked like sixty all day today and my brain is shrunk past rhyming. But I will say welcome to The Friendly Hour— *(Hugs IRENE)* —A club that lives up to its name.

IRENE: Oh God, oh God, oh God—Wava, I'm sorry about your face—! *(She bursts into tears and runs out of the house, barely stopping to grab her coat.)*

OPAL & WAVA: Irene!

DORCAS: Come back!

EFFIE: Heavens!

(They chase after IRENE, *ending up on the porch.)*

OPAL: We promise not to rhyme no more!

(Sounds of a car starting up and driving away. Wind sounds as well)

DORCAS: I meant horsey as a compliment!

(The car is gone. Silence for a moment.)

EFFIE: You shouldn't have hugged her.

DORCAS: Wava, what's wrong with your windmill?

WAVA: Marvin says the cable's broke, but he can't find the time to fix it.

DORCAS: I'll do it. *(Starts off)*

WAVA: No, Dorcas, we don't have a ladder long enough—

DORCAS: *(Disappearing)* Don't need a ladder.

EFFIE: Dorcas, you're not so spry as in high school—!

(Sound of a car approaching)

OPAL: Are you cuckoo?

WAVA: Marvin'll kill me for letting you up there!

EFFIE: Oh, no! She's climbing the windmill!

WAVA: Come down this instant! Oh, this is swell!

EFFIE: I can't watch! What if she falls?

(Covering her eyes, EFFIE *runs inside and hides in the closet. Sound of a car stopping)*

OPAL: Dorcas, look what you did to Effie!

WAVA: Is that Lucille?

(Sound of a car door slamming)

OPAL: Lucille, duck! Falling farm wives!

*(*LUCILLE *runs on the porch carrying an African violet and a Christmas gift. She gives both to* WAVA.)*

WAVA: Mercy! In the middle of winter! What is it?

OPAL: It's an African violet. Lucille, tell how you grow 'em so good.

(LUCILLE seems about to talk, but OPAL continues.)

OPAL: It's all about fertilizer. Not regular old cow manure like we have all over the place. Lucille's African violets need gazelle poop, but you can't get it here, so she uses sheep pellets, which is a good approximation—

WAVA: Oh!

(Looking up at DORCAS, the ladies cringe in unison.)

WAVA: Dorcas!

DORCAS: *(Distant)* I'm all right! Almost got it!

WAVA: I cannot watch her, and we don't want this to freeze. Come on in, girls.

(WAVA goes inside, but OPAL and LUCILLE stay out on the porch, fascinated with DORCAS' acrobatics on the windmill.)

WAVA: Effie?

(WAVA looks around for EFFIE, and sets the African violet somewhere everyone can see and adds the gift to the pile of presents.)

OPAL: They've always been a willful family. Dorcas and Wava's father took rat poison at the dinner table eight years ago. Made Wava and her mother sit there and finish dinner while he got all spasmodic— *(She demonstrates, arching her back.)* —And finally suffered respiratory arrest.

(WAVA opens the closet and finds EFFIE cowering there.)

WAVA: Effie, come out of there.

(WAVA drags EFFIE out of the closet.)

EFFIE: Is she down yet?

OPAL: Wava has to live with that memory all her life.

EFFIE: I'm sorry, Wava, I'm sorry. I'm such a chicken.

OPAL: Very nice, Dorcas, now get down from there before you blow off!

WAVA: *(Shows* EFFIE *the African violet)* Look what Lucille brought!

EFFIE: *(Sniffs)* Mmmm...they smell—like—

EFFIE & WAVA: *(Horrified)* —Cigars!

*(*EFFIE *and* WAVA *look at each other, stricken, then out to the porch.)*

WAVA: Effie, I'm losing my Christmas spirit. Can you play me a carol?

*(*WAVA *seats* EFFIE *at the piano and she plays* Jeg Er Saa Glad Hver Julekveld [I am so Glad Each Christmas Eve]. EFFIE *sings in Norwegian, alone at first.)*

DORCAS: *(Flushed from her climb)* That'll do for now.

OPAL: Indeed it will!

(The others join EFFIE *in song, but in English as she continues in Norwegian. All are singing loudly and vigorously, with a strong "swing" natural to the song. The minutes begin over the song as all begin to change clothes.* LUCILLE *quickly becomes* ISABELLE. *The piano may continue as a recording while* EFFIE *is changing or the song may be sung a capella.)*

DORCAS: *(Out)* Old carols were sung—

OPAL & WAVA: *(Out)* —And Secret Pals were revealed with one dollar Christmas gifts.

EFFIE: *(Out)* In our business meeting elections of officers were held.

OPAL: *(Out)* With Opal Zweifel as Treasurer.

DORCAS: *(Out)* Dorcas Briggle as secretary.

ISABELLE: *(Out)* Isabelle Hagen as Vice President.

EFFIE: *(Out)* And Effie Voss as President.

DORCAS: Again.

(They all look at her sharply, perhaps even pausing in their singing for a moment, then resuming.)

OPAL: *(Out, holding coin purse)* Treasurer's report: old balance—seventeen dollars and eighty-three cents. Dues:

(They each put a dime in the coin purse.)

OPAL: *(Out)* Fifty cents. New balance: eighteen dollars and thirty-three cents.

EFFIE: *(Out)* There being no further business—

DORCAS: *(Out)* The meeting was adjourned.

ALL: *(Out)* And a tasty lunch was served.

WAVA: *(Looking in the mirror and touching her red face.)* By hostess Wava Jamtgaard.

(They sing the carol's final verses in harmony as they finish changing. For the first time, EFFIE is not pregnant. ISABELLE makes a big deal out of turning on the electric lights. The song concludes.)

DORCAS: *(Appearing, out)* January 6, 1953. Our Friendly Hour Club met—

ISABELLE: *(Out)* —At da home of hostess Isabelle Hagen. *(Disappears into the kitchen.)*

WAVA: *(Appearing, out)* Six members were present for the roll call topic:

EFFIE: *(Appearing, out)* What to do on a snowy day. Opal Zweifel?

OPAL: Watch the children make snowmen—

WAVA: Snow angels!

DORCAS: Snowballs!

EFFIE: There better *not* be—!

(EFFIE *strides purposely to the door and flings it open. Sound of kids playing.*)

DORCAS: Oh, Effie, leave them be!

OPAL: Effie, the kids are fine!

EFFIE: *(Hollering out the door)* Verlyn—Howard—Norman—!

WAVA: Effie, you're letting the cold in!

EFFIE: No snowballs! For your own good! *(She closes the door and returns to the group.)* Wava Jamtgaard?

WAVA: Make hot cocoa and hope somebody visits.

EFFIE: Dorcas Briggle?

DORCAS: Hide from Clarence and—

DORCAS & EFFIE: —Read a book!

EFFIE: There's a surprise. Effie Voss? Bake cookies to warm up the kitchen. Irene DeSplinter?

IRENE: *(Appearing)* Ride my Blackie through the fields and listen to the silence as the snow absorbs all sound!

EFFIE: My, Irene, that's almost poetical!

IRENE: Wava's rubbing off on me!

WAVA: Irene, hush!

EFFIE: *(Loudly)* Isabelle Hagen?

ISABELLE: *(Hollering from the kitchen, recorded)* Tobogganing!

EFFIE: What?

ALL: Tobogganing!

OPAL: *(Out)* Wava Jamtgaard had charge of the craft and showed how to make cute little—

(WAVA *produces a cantaloupe-sized cellular sphere, decorated in white and gold.*)

EFFIE: What *is* that?

DORCAS: *(Out)* Easter ornaments. *(To* WAVA*)* It's an Easter ornament, isn't it, Wava?

WAVA: Made outta cut up— *(Reveals an armload of egg cartons)* Egg cartons. *(Passing out tools and materials)* See, you tie 'em together and it naturally forms a ball—

EFFIE: *(Skeptical)* Naturally.

DORCAS: Now, Effie.

OPAL: It's darling!

IRENE: Oh, I get it.

DORCAS: You're a chatauqua kind of gal.

OPAL: I think crafts are fun.

IRENE: Me, too!

WAVA: I love 'em!

(They all start working on the craft, EFFIE *somewhat reluctantly.)*

DORCAS: They can go on the table for Easter dinner—

WAVA: Or on the door—

IRENE: Blackie might want to wear one—

OPAL: Take 'em to church—

DORCAS: Sure!

IRENE: How do you—?

WAVA: *(Helping* IRENE*)* Here, you just—

IRENE: Oh, I see.

(They all work in silence for a moment. EFFIE *sighs, and maybe even stops her halfhearted attempt to piece together the Easter ball.)*

OPAL: Birthday reminder.

DORCAS: Opal, it's weeks away.

IRENE: Who?

WAVA: Next meeting—

OPAL: I'll bring a cake!

EFFIE: Forty one?

DORCAS: How nice, Effie, you remember *exactly*.

EFFIE: It's okay for me to say, 'cause I'm older still.

DORCAS: Opal, shouldn't we be paying dues?

EFFIE: What an interesting change of subject. And not your favorite, either.

OPAL & WAVA: Effie!

IRENE: *(Getting up)* Do you think Isabelle has any nut picks?

OPAL: *(Digging in her purse)* Lemme get the— where's—?

WAVA: Good idea—Isabelle has everything.

(IRENE goes into the kitchen.)

OPAL: *(Getting up)* I musta left the treasury in the car.

(OPAL runs out. Sound of kids)

DORCAS: I gave our treasury to the American Communist Party.

EFFIE: Not funny. Not!

WAVA: Dorcas, you didn't!

DORCAS: I enrolled us all, and our official cards are coming in six weeks.

EFFIE: This is not the time to be joking about such things.

WAVA: You couldn't possibly!

(OPAL returns with the coin purse. Sound of kids outside)

OPAL: *(Hollering)* Isabelle, you tear down your outhouse?

ISABELLE: *(Hollering from the kitchen) Ja!* Mister Elgerma tear it down!

WAVA: Isabelle is so modern!

OPAL: They're Hollanders, but the best neighbors you could ask for.

DORCAS: They got a— *(Gestures toward a door)*

OPAL: *(Going to the bathroom door)* Effie, do you care if Verlyn sleds on top of the barn?

EFFIE: *(Jumping up)* Sleds?! On the barn!?

(EFFIE runs out onto the porch. OPAL steps into the bathroom.)

OPAL: Well, look at that!

EFFIE: Verlyn! One!

(Sound of the toilet flushing)

EFFIE: Two!

OPAL: Come look at this!

DORCAS: Opal, we've all seen—

(DORCAS and WAVA go to the bathroom door. Sound of kids outside)

EFFIE: Three!

OPAL: But this is Isabelle's!

EFFIE: You're making your poor mother freeze!

(EFFIE stalks off to take care of Verlyn. Sound of the toilet flushing.)

WAVA: Marvin says we'll get a septic tank this summer.

DORCAS: Very nice.

OPAL: *(Confidentially as they return to their seats)* Effie's not so hot on crafts, is she?

WAVA: Well, not everybody—

DORCAS: Gwenneth inherited Wava's talent—four blue ribbons at the state fair—

(Barely audible sounds of EFFIE *and the kids arguing.)*

OPAL: Even so, Effie should be more cordial about it to you, Wava. Look. *((Holds up* EFFIE'*s craft, which is wadded together badly)* Time somebody said something. *(Looks pointedly at* DORCAS*)*

DORCAS: Opal, Effie for sure gets under my skin, but she's also as loyal—

WAVA: And honest!

DORCAS: —As a friend can be.

WAVA: She's generous to her friends, too.

DORCAS: And nobody's better at keeping a secret.

OPAL: Like I say—

*(*LUCILLE *comes in with a houseplant.)*

WAVA: We all got faults, Opal.

OPAL: Don't I know it!

(The kids outside suddenly holler, and EFFIE *screams.)*

DORCAS: Oh, that Verlyn! Gwenneth says her teacher calls him the devil!

*(*DORCAS, OPAL, *and* WAVA *brush by* LUCILLE *as they run out the door. Moments later,* EFFIE *dashes inside and hides in the closet.* LUCILLE *sets down the plant where everyone can see, and goes into the kitchen. After a moment,* DORCAS *comes back inside, her dress stained with fresh blood. She stands outside the closet door.)*

DORCAS: Effie, you come out of there.

EFFIE: I couldn't possibly.

DORCAS: Verlyn's an awful sight, bleeding like slaughtering day, but nothing seems broken.

(DORCAS *opens the closet door, and* EFFIE *is facing the back of the closet.*)

DORCAS: Wava's taking care of him.

EFFIE: (*Turning around*) She's good at that.

(EFFIE *sees the blood on* DORCAS' *dress, screams, jumps back in the closet, and pulls the door shut behind her.*)

DORCAS: Effie, he's all right. Just not so smart. Go out and see him. I'll go with you.

EFFIE: (*Opening the door*) You will?

DORCAS: 'Course! (*Taking* EFFIE's *arm*) Let's go.

ISABELLE: (*Appears in an apron, out*) Effie's Verlyn cut his head in a fall off the barn, but we got him patched up all right.

OPAL: (*Out*) Our meeting resumed with a letter Effie received—

ISABELLE, OPAL, & WAVA: (*Out*) From The White House!

EFFIE: (*Appears, reading*) The Office of the President. Dear Mrs Voss: President Eisenhower has asked me to express his thanks to you and members of The Friendly Hour Club for your very kind message.

(*The ladies begin to change their clothes.*)

WAVA: (*Reading*) It was thoughtful of you to wire, and the President wants me to assure you of his gratitude for your good wishes for his trip to the Far East.

ISABELLE: (*Reading*) With the President's best wishes to each of you,

EFFIE: (*Reading*) Sincerely yours, Wilton B Persons.

EFFIE & OPAL: (*Out*) Two dollars were sent—

EFFIE: *(Out)* As a memorial gift to the Kristensen family on the death of their mother.

DORCAS & EFFIE: *(Out)* There being no further business old or new—

EFFIE, OPAL, & WAVA: *(Out)* The meeting was adjourned.

ALL: *(Out)* And a tasty lunch was served.

ISABELLE: *(Out)* By hostess Isabelle Hagen.

EFFIE: *(Out)* February 5, 1963. Our Club met at the home of—

OPAL: *(Out, quickly)* Lucille Ostensen.

WAVA: *(Looking around the room, which is filled with plants and flowers.)* Mercy! It's so clean!

DORCAS: Where's Lucille?

ISABELLE: In de kitchen. I go get her.

EFFIE: Wait, Isabelle! Roll call.

DORCAS: Most embarrassing moment! Isabelle?

ISABELLE: You were all there! When I made dat anga food cake with the cracked egg—

OPAL: And we were puking all night!

ISABELLE: And everybody got sick!

WAVA: Oh, Isabelle, it wasn't that bad.

(Clearly not everyone agrees with WAVA.)

ISABELLE: *(Going into the kitchen)* Lucille, I will help!

DORCAS: Opal Zweifel?

OPAL: I guess I can't complain too much, because I haven't done anything about it, but I was just mortified when they put up the sign for my beauty parlor and it said "Lady Bug Beauty Saloon".

WAVA: Nobody even notices any more.

DORCAS: Wava Jamtgaard?

WAVA: Oh, Dorcas, I couldn't possibly.

EFFIE: Wava, you don't wanna be marked absent.

DORCAS: Effie Voss?

EFFIE: Wait, I really think—

DORCAS: Maybe this wasn't the best roll call topic for everyone—

EFFIE: Well, of course, it's embarrassing. It's supposed to be. Mine's awful. And recent. Remember last year I told everyone we were going to Norway?

OPAL: Oh, that's right.

EFFIE: And then you'll notice we never went. Walter decided at the last minute we couldn't afford it.

DORCAS: That must've frosted you.

EFFIE: Did it ever! Now, Wava—

DORCAS: Dorcas Briggle? My worst moment was when I went to get a Social Security card and they needed a birth certificate. I was born so late—

WAVA: Ma was forty-three—

DORCAS: That no one ever bothered to get me one. Like I didn't even exist. And I didn't get in the family portrait, either.

WAVA: But Marvin saved you.

DORCAS: That's right, my brother vouched for me and I got my card. None of the rest of you know how awful it is to be last born. My father wouldn't let me have piano lessons or college—

WAVA: That's 'cause you were so popular he knew you'd get married.

DORCAS: Was college a waste of money for you, Effie?

EFFIE: I cherish the memories—

DORCAS: And you remember every bit of it!

EFFIE: Now—most embarrassing moment—

EFFIE: Wava Jamtgaard?

DORCAS: Irene DeSplinter?

IRENE: *(Appearing)* I think it's *right now!* Where's Lucille's bathroom?

(They all point. IRENE *runs into the bathroom.)*

EFFIE: Heavens! I hope we're not all gonna get the stomach flu!

OPAL: Irene hasn't been right since Bob passed away.

WAVA: So sad.

EFFIE: What was it, really?

DORCAS: I understand.

OPAL: They said dropsy, but—

EFFIE: Well...

OPAL: She told me on his deathbed he *said* he didn't believe in God. Then gave a little "oh" and was gone.

EFFIE: He *was* Catholic.

WAVA: What an awful blow!

DORCAS: I wonder what he did believe in.

EFFIE: Sounds like nothing.

WAVA: Oh, you have to believe in something!

OPAL: I think he believed in— *(Mimes a bottle)*

EFFIE: Opal, that's unkind, if probably true.

DORCAS: If there's no God, why live? I wouldn't know what to do or why to do it.

WAVA: Dorcas, don't be awful.

DORCAS: If I didn't believe in God, I'd just want to kill myself.

EFFIE: *(Warningly)* Religion.

DORCAS: Sorry, Effie, I forgot. But I sometimes wish we'd talk about—

EFFIE: *(Out)* Our guest was—

(EDNA appears wearing very youthful, mod, 60s clothes, with long straight hair. She wields an electric knife.)

EDNA: *(Oklahoma accent, out.)* Edna Patton, Home Services Advisor for the Rural Electrification Association—

EFFIE & WAVA: *(Out)* To demonstrate—

EDNA: *(Out)* How to use an electric knife— *(She whirrs the knife.)*

DORCAS & OPAL: *(Out)* And—

EDNA: *(Out)* How to freeze food.

OPAL: You're from the South, aren't you?

EDNA: I'm from Ardmore, Oklahoma—

(They all catch their breath as if to sing.)

EDNA: —And please don't sing. It's the first thing everybody does.

EFFIE: Well, it's a catchy song.

DORCAS: Gwenneth played Aunt Eller at South Dakota State.

(EFFIE reacts.)

OPAL: Your accent is so cute. Say "How now, brown cow."

EDNA: *(Reluctantly)* How now, brown cow.

EFFIE & OPAL: *(Imitating EDNA)* How now, brown cow.

OPAL: I just love it!

DORCAS: I'm so concerned about freezer burn.

(EDNA *demonstrates with ground meat, wax paper, and aluminum foil.*)

EDNA: Layers'll save you. First the wax paper, folded like this to seal the meat in, then aluminum foil to hold the whole package together. Tight, tight, tight!

OPAL: I have a new deep freeze nearly full.

EDNA: Everyone should get one. Imagine sweet corn all winter long!

WAVA: Without drying?

DORCAS: Doesn't the electricity cost a lot for a big deep freeze, Opal?

EDNA: Oh, pennies, that's all!

OPAL: But it's worth it, don'tcha know.

EDNA: *(Whirring the knife)* Now, what can I cut?

WAVA: Come with me to the kitchen, Edna.

(Taking EDNA *with her.)*

WAVA: Maybe Lucille has something needs dicing for lunch.

(For just a moment, DORCAS, EFFIE, *and* OPAL *sip coffee. Then suddenly:)*

EFFIE: I wonder why Wava—?

OPAL: Wava's embarrassing—

DORCAS: Girls, drop it.

EFFIE: Dorcas, no need to be curt.

DORCAS: Effie, you of all people should guess—

EFFIE: Ohh.

DORCAS: Yes.

OPAL: What? Does it have to do with a certain fiddle player?

(Sound of the electric knife in the kitchen, perhaps appreciative exclamations.)

DORCAS: Believe it or not, Opal, there are some things even you don't need to know.

OPAL: Like I say, I didn't mean—

WAVA: *(Coming back in)* Lucille made some of her dark bread, and Edna's just slicing away like magic.

(All of them quietly sip their coffee.)

OPAL: I hope Irene is all right. *(Calls)* Irene!

IRENE: *(From the bathroom)* Just a minute!

OPAL: I have some Kaopectate in the car.

(No response)

OPAL: Pepto Bismol, too.

(No response.)

OPAL: When I get the trots, which is fairly frequent but not as frequent as the opposite problem—

EFFIE: Opal Zweifel, you never wanna talk about anything but poop. Poop, poop, poop is all that ever comes out of your mouth. For your own good, you need to grow up and admit some other topic to your vocabulary. I take back my most embarrassing moment—it's now, or any time you go on about BMs and other intestinal matters. We just don't need to hear it. If we want that kind of talk, we all have children— well, most of us, Wava—

WAVA: Oh, I knew what you meant—

EFFIE: That's just not what we come to club for.

(Silence for a moment)

DORCAS: I don't mind when Opal—

EFFIE: Well, I do!

DORCAS: It's perfectly normal and healthy to—

EFFIE: And who's President of this club?!

EDNA: *(Coming out of the kitchen with a plate of sliced bread.)* Here you go—best thing since sliced bread!

(No one reacts.)

EDNA: Sliced bread!

WAVA: Oh, Edna, how marvelous! Perfectly cut! Each one exactly the same.

EDNA: The electric miracle!

OPAL: Kaopectate's a kind of miracle.

EFFIE: Opal Zweifel—!

DORCAS: Now, Effie, don't—

EDNA: Excuse me, but what's—

EFFIE: You are the stubbornest, gossipiest—

WAVA: Oh, girls, please don't quarrel—

OPAL: Gossipiest?!

DORCAS: Effie, not everybody has to do your mighty will one hundred percent of the time—

WAVA: I can't bear it!

EDNA: Looks like my job here is done.

EFFIE: Dorcas Briggle, you find Opal's talk as smutty as I do, but you're taking her side just to frost me—!

EDNA: Enjoy your slices!

OPAL: I'm not smutty! I'm scatalogical!

WAVA: Oh, wait, Edna—

(EDNA leaves quickly.)

EFFIE: None of you even know how to use big words properly—

DORCAS: Contrary to your belief, Effie Voss, I do not sit around all day thinking about you and your miseries—

(WAVA *suddenly starts wailing like a loon.*)

EFFIE: Miseries! You're the one with miseries, only I won't stoop to naming 'em—

OPAL: Just because you're the only one went to college—

(DORCAS *starts quacking like a duck.*)

EFFIE: It's that Congregational church, I'm certain—

(OPAL *starts cawing like a crow.*)

EFFIE: No restrictions on what folks say any more—

(*From the kitchen* LUCILLE *can be heard doing her sloughpumper sound.*)

EFFIE: Anything goes—

(*They are all quiet for a moment, listening to the strange sound of the sloughpumper in the kitchen.*)

EFFIE: —These days—

(EFFIE *is quiet once again as the sound of* ISABELLE *imitating a mourning dove floats in from the kitchen. After a moment the sloughpumper starts up again, too.*)

EFFIE: It's just—

(*Everyone makes their bird sounds all at once, and* EFFIE *joins them at last with her meadowlark call. After a moment or two of this cacophony,* IRENE *pops out of the bathroom and makes a piercing hawk cry, adding to the chaos.* WAVA *starts to laugh, still rather like a loon.*)

EFFIE: (*Out, over the bird calls*) We voted to make a gift—

IRENE & WAVA: (*Out*) Of five dollars—

(IRENE *disappears.*)

EFFIE & OPAL: (*Out*) To the Gustafsons—

(*One by one, they stop making bird calls.*)

OPAL: (*Out, knowingly*) Whose house burnt down.

EFFIE: *(Out)* There being no further business—

DORCAS, EFFIE, & OPAL: *(Out)* Old or new—

(The bird calls have all ceased.)

DORCAS & OPAL: *(Out)* We practiced bird calls—

WAVA: *(Out, laughing)* Some of which we hadn't heard for years!

EFFIE: *(Out, irritated at the interruption)* Our business meeting adjourned—

ALL: *(Out)* And a tasty lunch was served—

OPAL: *(Out)* By hostess Lucille Ostensen.

(The ladies quietly begin singing That Easter Day with Joy was Bright *in harmony as they change clothes. After a verse or two:)*

DORCAS & EFFIE: *(Out)* Our Friendly Hour Club met on March—

EFFIE: Fourth—

DORCAS: Fifth—

EFFIE: Fourth—

DORCAS: Are you sure?

EFFIE: Fourth! Tuesday, March fourth—

DORCAS: Oh, of course! You're right.

ALL: Nineteen sixty-nine.

WAVA: *(Out)* At the home of—

ALL: New member—

ELVERA: *(Out)* Elvera Norman. *(She wears a cardigan and has gray hair.)*

DORCAS: *(Out)* With eight members present—

EFFIE: *(Out)* Six.

OPAL: *(Counting on fingers)* Me, Effie, Dorcas, Wava, Elvera, Isabelle—

DORCAS: *(Out)* Eight members present—

EFFIE: Lucille and Irene were not present for roll call.

OPAL: *(Counting)* Irene, Lucille—

WAVA: But they came!

EFFIE: Late!

OPAL: This is the biggest we've ever been!

DORCAS: *(Out)* For the roll call question:

DORCAS & WAVA: *(Out)* What would you say to God if you met Him?

EFFIE: We're all going to meet Him.

DORCAS: In heaven, *ja* sure—but if you met him now.

EFFIE: Go right ahead as you always do, but I am voicing my discomfort with this question.

DORCAS: Elvera Norman?

ELVERA: Thank you for the world, I think, yes, that's what I'd say. There's so much in it, so much to see, every little thing is precious if you look long enough, and God made it all. Thank you, God!

DORCAS: What a beautiful answer, Elvera. Effie, are you still discomforted?

EFFIE: *Discomfited*, and I still am.

DORCAS: Effie, must you *always* correct my pronounciation?

ELVERA: Excuse me, I have to get the— *(She leaves.)*

EFFIE: Pro*nun*ciation!

WAVA: I would thank God, excuse me—

DORCAS: Opal Zweifel?

OPAL: I would ask God—

DORCAS: Wava?

WAVA: No, Opal, go ahead—

OPAL: I would ask God why he took our Amy so young.

EFFIE: Opal, that was terrible, but you can't ask that!

WAVA: Oh, Opal, I would, too!

OPAL: She was only four. Palmer's never been the same since.

EFFIE: God had his reasons, I'm sure.

OPAL: I will never understand!

EFFIE: We're not meant to understand. That's for God. *(Glaring)* Dorcas!

DORCAS: Oh, my turn?

EFFIE: That's why you asked it, I'm sure—

WAVA: Excuse me, I thought it was mine—

DORCAS: Wava Jamtgaard?

WAVA: Don't worry, Effie, I know we're meant to suffer in this life, so I'm not—I won't—I would only thank God—like Elvera—for my wonderful friends. I don't know what I'd do without The Friendly Hour to look forward to every month. I'd just shut myself in my room and close the door forever!

DORCAS: Isabelle Hagen?

ISABELLE: *(Appearing)* I would say *tack sa mycket* to God for this country.

OPAL & WAVA: Ohhh!

ISABELLE: When I first come I spoke no English. I didn't fit. But America made room for me. I dream sometimes of Sweden, but here is home.

EFFIE: And you're celebrating a birthday soon!

ISABELLE: Oh! Effie! Dat I am not so happy about! And
it's not until August. *(Calling, as she goes in the kitchen)*
Elvera, you need help?

EFFIE & OPAL: *(Confidentially)* Sixty!

WAVA: Mercy!

DORCAS: Effie Voss?

EFFIE: What?

DORCAS: You're not yet present.

EFFIE: Oh, very well. I talk to God many times every
day, so I don't really have anything new to say to Him.
But I truly do look forward to seeing Him face to face.
The moment we all live for.

DORCAS: Dorcas Briggle?

EFFIE: Here we go.

DORCAS: Now, Effie, I don't know what you're nervous
I'll say. Afraid I'll embarrass God with an impertinent
question—?

EFFIE: You embarrass everyone else.

DORCAS: Sometimes your God seems so different
from my God, more Old Testament, if you don't mind
me saying. If God is God, what question could make
Him blush or cause upset? God is better than we are,
not all jealous and, well, even petty like in Genesis or
Exodus—

EFFIE: Dorcas Briggle, you're a Gnostic!

DORCAS: I am not! What's that?

EFFIE: It's a heresy is what that is. Do you think there
are two Gods, a different one for each Testament?

DORCAS: No!

WAVA: Dorcas isn't a heretic!

OPAL: What an exciting meeting, and we're not even through Roll Call.

DORCAS: If you'd just let me answer, I'd only thank God for Gwenneth. She just got promoted at the wildlife refuge.

EFFIE: You might wanna ask him to help you overcome pride.

WAVA: Effie!

OPAL: Oh, my!

DORCAS: I only have the one, not six to keep track of like some people.

EFFIE: She's a tomboy and practically a hippie.

DORCAS: But I am proud of Gwenneth. I admit it.

WAVA: Well, if Dorcas is guilty of the sin of pride, then I admit to envy. You are all so lucky to have children!

OPAL: Oh, yes!

WAVA: All I have is Marvin.

EFFIE: Your brother is very good to you.

OPAL: Wonder why he never got married....

DORCAS: *(Out)* For the entertainment, Elvera showed us her rock collection.

ELVERA: *(With a box of rocks)* I found this quartz crystal down by the crick.

WAVA: Beautiful!

OPAL: It's perfectly shaped!

ELVERA: And this is a petrified rose.

DORCAS: I didn't know that could happen!

EFFIE: That's something!

ELVERA: Amethyst.

DORCAS: Oooh!

EFFIE: Lavender!

WAVA: How pretty!

OPAL: You had to buy that one, didn't you?

ELVERA: I found most of 'em, but some I get mail-order.
I found this one, and it would be hard to buy.

WAVA: What is it?

OPAL: Just looks like an old bone.

ELVERA: It's a fossil mammal—

EFFIE: A fossil!

ELVERA: From the Pleistocene Era.

WAVA: What kind of mammal?

OPAL: Oh, it's just a buffalo—

ELVERA: Megatherium, I think, a giant—

DORCAS: What's Pleistocene?

ELVERA: The Ice Age—forty thousand years—

EFFIE: Now, Elvera, those fossils were just planted
there to confuse us.

ELVERA: Planted?

EFFIE: They're not that old at all—

DORCAS: By who?

EFFIE: By the devil.

ELVERA: *(Sweetly)* Oh, I have to show Isabelle how to
turn off my oven. It's got a mind of its own! *(Runs out)*

(Everyone sips coffee.)

WAVA: Umm...

EFFIE: What?

WAVA: Oh...nothing. I wonder if we'll be able to see the
spaceship tonight.

EFFIE: Oh, Wava, it's way too small for the naked eye.

DORCAS: They're testing the Lunar Module.

OPAL: I heard you *could* see Apollo.

(They sip coffee.)

OPAL: Have you heard about the Sorensons?

WAVA: Oh, dear.

OPAL: Yes, it's true. Hard to believe.

DORCAS: Divorce?

(OPAL nods, gravely.)

EFFIE: Really? I didn't want to believe it.

DORCAS: I move that we send Earline a gift.

OPAL: Money?

EFFIE: A *divorce* gift?

DORCAS: She's going to need it.

EFFIE: Then she'll know we know.

WAVA: I don't know any divorced people.

OPAL: Oh, sure, there's—

EFFIE: Opal.

WAVA: We don't know anyone *well*.

OPAL: Dorcas, you know she's the one divorcing *him*.

DORCAS: Oh. But—

EFFIE: It just wouldn't be right.

WAVA: Wouldn't want to embarrass her.

EFFIE: She should pray to save her marriage like—

WAVA: We could pray *for* her.

IRENE: *(Coming in from the kitchen with a coffee pot)* More coffee, anyone?

DORCAS: Never mind. I'll do it myself.

EFFIE: What?

IRENE: Do what?

DORCAS: I'll give her a little something. Don't worry about it.

IRENE: Okay, I won't. What?

EFFIE: Our business meeting is over, don't you think?

WAVA: *(Out)* No business—

EFFIE: *(Out)* Old or new—

DORCAS: *(Out)* New or old—

DORCAS & EFFIE: Sorry—

DORCAS: No—

EFFIE: Go ahead—

ALL: *(Out)* So the meeting was adjourned.

IRENE: *(Out)* Effie Voss had the entertainment—

EFFIE: *(Out)* Which was a contest—

DORCAS: What *kind* of contest?

EFFIE: It's called "Number, Please." All the answers are numbers.

OPAL: We haven't had a good contest in a while.

DORCAS & EFFIE: No, we haven't. *(They look at each other.)*

IRENE: Gotta trot—Elvera needs me. *(Disappears into the kitchen.)*

OPAL: What's the first question?

DORCAS: I don't want to play a contest. It's silly.

EFFIE: Remember each answer is a number—
Silly?

WAVA: Dorcas, please. Effie, go on.

OPAL: We used to have contests all the time.

EFFIE: What did Alice do when she saw the cookies?

(Silence for a moment)

OPAL: You know, if Dorcas doesn't want to—

EFFIE: Eight one!

DORCAS: I don't.

WAVA: What?

EFFIE: *(Drawing numbers in the air)* She "ate one!"

OPAL: Oh. Well, isn't that clever? See, Dorcas, it's not so bad.

(DORCAS *glowers but says nothing.*)

EFFIE: That's right, it's cute and fun. Second question, and you all should try to answer this time—

ISABELLE: *(Coming out of the kitchen)* I must to go now.

WAVA: Oh, no, Isabelle!

OPAL: Already?

DORCAS: Just when we're starting to have fun?

ISABELLE: *(Sensing the tension)* Ja, I go. *Hejda!*

ALL: *Hejda!*

(ISABELLE *goes out the front door. Silence for a moment)*

EFFIE: How did the ballerina spend her allowance?

(Silence)

WAVA: This is hard.

DORCAS: *(Getting up)* With Isabelle gone, I bet Elvera needs help—

OPAL: Oh, Dorcas, stay—

EFFIE: This is an official Friendly Hour activity—

OPAL: Effie, we can't *make* Dorcas have fun—

DORCAS: I'm all for fun, just not—

EFFIE: We play contests *together*—that's what's nice about our club—

WAVA: What was the question again?

EFFIE: How did the ballerina spent her allowance?

(They sip coffee.)

EFFIE: Ballerina....?

OPAL: Dorcas, you're so smart, reading all those books. If anyone can figure it out, you can.

(DORCAS just looks exasperated.)

EFFIE: It's not that hard.

(No response)

EFFIE: Heavens!

(No response)

EFFIE: Four one two two!

WAVA: What?

DORCAS: Oh.

EFFIE: For one tu-tu! You know, a ballet skirt—

OPAL: Cute! Dorcas, don't be such a grumpy-gus with Effie!

WAVA: She spent her allowance for one tu-tu!

DORCAS: Sorry, Effie. That was very clever.

(ELVERA comes out of the kitchen with a plate of treats.)

OPAL: And, Effie, on your part, if Dorcas prefers—

EFFIE: Opal Zweifel, you are only exacerbating the situation!

(ELVERA sets down the plate of treats and fairly runs back to the kitchen. OPAL compulsively starts eating the treats.)

DORCAS: Exacerbating!

WAVA: Mercy!

EFFIE: I know you are well-meaning, but its not lost on me how you poke at each of us in your instigating way—

DORCAS: Instigating!

EFFIE: Almost as if you *want* us to fuss at each other.

OPAL: *(Standing)* I wonder what Elvera's planned for dessert. *(Heads to the kitchen)* I was only trying to help, don'tcha know.

WAVA: Effie...

DORCAS: Wava, don't—

WAVA: Dorcas, somebody has to—!

EFFIE: Somebody has to what?

WAVA: Opal's in a bit of a state just now. We all thought she didn't notice about Palmer—saying things—

DORCAS: Making passes, if we're speaking plain.

WAVA: —To other ladies. But she does notice, she told me. She does.

EFFIE: That is in part her fault. Dessert is the last thing she needs.

WAVA: It's glandular!

DORCAS: Effie, that is unkind!

EFFIE: I am not unkind. I am straightforward. And Wava, you are always trying to smooth things over, and I appreciate that about you, but right now—

DORCAS: *(Overlapping)* Yes, I've always appreciated that about you—

EFFIE: —At this very moment you are sounding an awful lot like Opal, spreading gossip and betraying a confidence—

WAVA: Betraying!

DORCAS: Effie Voss! That is quite enough. You will not talk to my sister that way ever again. No one in the world is more genuine and caring than Wava, and you've known it all your life. Everyone loves her, and you're just jealous, which is why you always insist on your own way in religion and politics and especially in The Friendly Hour.

(IRENE and OPAL come out of the kitchen. When she sees what's going on, IRENE tries to retreat, but OPAL grabs her.)

DORCAS: Nobody can be right but you, and if we have fun it's got to be your kind of fun, like ridiculous contests you know you can always win. I'm sorry, Effie, but Wava's right, somebody has to—you just can't—something has to change, and being nicer to Wava would be a start!

EFFIE: Dorcas Briggle, I know you and Wava have had a hard life, with your father's troubles and Clarence being so peevish and all, but I have been remarkably kind to Wava under the circumstances—

WAVA: What circumstances?!

EFFIE: As you well know— 'Cause you're the one who told me thirty-seven years ago that Wava got her face burnt to a crisp by Doctor Hoard—

DORCAS: Effie, stop—please—

EFFIE: —When she had her eye on my Walter—

DORCAS: That was before he was yours!

EFFIE: So it seems betraying a confidence just runs in your family along with tomboy hippies and suicide!

(They all stare at EFFIE a moment while she realizes what she has done.)

EFFIE: Oh!

(EFFIE runs into the closet and slams the door behind her.)

DORCAS: Wava—

WAVA: *(Standing)* You...told...?

DORCAS: It was so long ago—I thought it would—we were girls—

(Her hand to her mouth, WAVA runs out of the house. IRENE dashes after her.)

IRENE: Wava, hold your horses—!

DORCAS: Wava, please!

OPAL: *(After a moment)* Don't worry, Dorcas. She's your only sister! And your best friend, too, if you think about it. I'm sure she'll speak to you again. Eventually.

(DORCAS just sits, sipping coffee, staring into space. OPAL goes to the closet door and knocks.)

OPAL: Effie, come out of there.

(No response)

OPAL: It's getting dark. Maybe we'll be able to see the Apollo. I heard it's bright enough you can, as long as the moon isn't up.

(No response)

OPAL: Dorcas, don't just sit there drinking Elvera's coffee. I don't know why you didn't run after your sister. Tell Effie you didn't mean it, or if that's not true at least say you're sorry.

(No response. OPAL goes to the kitchen.)

OPAL: Elvera, I could use a little help out here!

ELVERA: *(From the kitchen)* I'm cooking!

OPAL: *(Back to the closet door)* Effie, if you don't come out of there, this could be the last meeting of The Friendly Hour. If you give up on the contests, I'm sure Dorcas'll stop trying to make us read books we don't like. Effie? Come on, Effie!

(Suddenly EFFIE *flings open the closet door and steps out, trembling with anger. They stare at her a moment.)*

EFFIE: I don't believe in evolution!

*(*EFFIE *runs out of the house just as* LUCILLE *is approaching with a plant.)*

OPAL: Effie! *(Grabbing* DORCAS*)* Dorcas, we can't let her run away, too. Don't be so prideful! *(Dragging* DORCAS *toward the kitchen)* Good-bye, Elvera!

DORCAS: Good-bye!

ELVERA: *(From the kitchen)* But what about lunch?!

*(*DORCAS *and* OPAL *dash past* LUCILLE *and disappear.* LUCILLE *is left on the porch, confused.)*

ELVERA: Opal? Dorcas? Effie?

*(*LUCILLE *squints up toward the sky.)*

ELVERA: I've got an Easter ham, scalloped potatoes, my mother's homemade rolls, corn, beets, pickles, black olives, ambrosia, bundt cake—

*(*LUCILLE *sees the Apollo spacecraft.)*

ELVERA: —An a new tollhouse cookie recipe! Opal? Girls?

END OF ACT ONE

ACT TWO

OPAL: *(Appearing, out)* Our Friendly Hour Club met at the home of—

DORCAS: *(Appearing, out)* Dorcas Briggle.

ELVERA: *(Appearing, out)* On April 2, 1974.

DORCAS, ELVERA, & OPAL: With three members present—

(All three ladies have the exact same hairstyle.)

OPAL: *(Out)* —For the roll call question:

DORCAS: *(Out)* What do you think of Watergate? Elvera Norman?

ELVERA: Oh, Dorcas, haven't we heard enough about that?

DORCAS: Opal Zweifel?

OPAL: Don't blame me. I voted for McGovern.

DORCAS: Good for you.

ELVERA: Really, Opal?

OPAL: He's a little "out there," but imagine if we'd had a South Dakotan in the White House.

DORCAS: Dorcas Briggle? I think it's going to get worse before it gets better but I hope our country can come back together after this terrible time. And yes, I think the President knew all along.

ELVERA: Don't let Effie hear you say that!

DORCAS: Effie isn't likely to hear me say anything, is she?

ELVERA: No, I guess not.

OPAL: *(Out)* Lucille Ostensen had company from Minnesota—

DORCAS, ELVERA, & OPAL: *(Out)* —And was absent.

OPAL: *(Out)* Elvera had charge of the entertainment.

DORCAS: *(Out)* And showed us her ant farm.

ELVERA: *(Showing a plastic ant farm)* Look how busy they all are—gathering food, which is sugar water, making tunnels, tending the pupae—that's the eggs. And they're all taking care of the one queen. Isn't that interesting?

(Lighting shift isolates ELVERA *from* DORCAS *and* OPAL.*)*

OPAL: Effie's mad you're still calling this the Friendly Hour Club.

ELVERA: Not everybody thinks ants are all that interesting.

DORCAS: I wish she'd find something else to be mad about. It's been five years!

ELVERA: Why should their tiny lives matter to us? What could be more ordinary than an ant?

DORCAS: I'll just have to outlive her.

ELVERA: But if you look close enough, even an ant can be interesting.

OPAL: I think Irene would like to come back to this Friendly Hour Club, and I know Wava wants to.

ELVERA: See that one trying to move that ball of sand all by herself? All the workers are female, by the way. Oh, look! Her friends are coming to help her. Isn't that interesting?

DORCAS: *(Out)* Opal read a letter from Isabelle in Colorado—

OPAL: *(Out)* While we did a craft activity—

DORCAS, ELVERA, & OPAL: *(Out)* Net poodles—

ELVERA: *(Out)* That was Dorcas' idea.

(They make net poodles.)

OPAL: *(Reading)* Dear Girls: Thank you for the *lefse* you sent for my birthday, so nice to have that reminder of home or should I say "old home" as Ragnar is happy here in Colorado Springs except for the mountains that made us so nervous the first night we had to go out east and stay in a motel, guess we miss the plains—

(Lights isolate OPAL from DORCAS and ELVERA.)

ELVERA: Did you really tear down those outbuildings by yourself?

OPAL: —But we enjoy being near the grandchildren of course—

DORCAS: I got tired of waiting for Clarence to do it or hire someone.

OPAL: —And Kristen comes by almost every day so I make her a little lunch—

DORCAS: With no Holsteins that milkhouse was a waste of land—

OPAL: —Which reminds me of The Friendly Hour Club—

DORCAS: And I was tired of the rats under the chicken house—

OPAL: —Nothing like that here in Colorado I think of you every day—

DORCAS: *(Out)* We enjoyed our book discussion of—

DORCAS, ELVERA, & OPAL: *(With various reactions)* The *Exorcist.*

ELVERA: I just kept thinking of Effie the whole time— the language—!

OPAL: She's got us reading *The Late Great Planet Earth* in the other Friendly Hour Club.

DORCAS: I knew she'd come around to that book idea.

OPAL: I'm afraid to see the movie.

ELVERA: I couldn't read it at night!

DORCAS: But weren't the theological discussions interesting?

OPAL: Sure.

ELVERA: I guess...

OPAL: Palmer got a hold of mine and underlined all the dirty words.

DORCAS: *(Out)* In honor of the 25th Anniversary of the Lady Bug Beauty Saloon, Opal gave us—

DORCAS, ELVERA, & OPAL: *(Out)* —All the same hairstyle.

ELVERA: *(Out)* Effie Voss's mother passed away, so we voted to give—

DORCAS: *(Out)* Twenty-five dollars—

ELVERA: Twenty-five!

OPAL: Dorcas, we only have twenty-seven dollars in the whole treasury—

DORCAS: We need to catch up with inflation. I move we increase dues to twenty-five cents a month.

DORCAS & ELVERA: Twenty-five!

DORCAS: *(Out)* —To the Voss family as a memorial gift.

ELVERA: *(Out)* Opal brought a special dessert—

DORCAS: Oh, let me get it. *(Disappears)*

OPAL: Does Dorcas seem out of sorts to you?

ELVERA: No, but I haven't known her as long.

OPAL: I think it's because Gwenneth—no, never mind—

ELVERA: Gwenneth what?

OPAL: No, I only heard, don'tcha know—

ELVERA: What about Gwenneth?

OPAL: Well. I heard she was gonna have a baby and now she's not.

ELVERA: Oh, how sad—she lost it?

OPAL: Not exactly.

ELVERA: Oh. Ohh!

OPAL: She's not married.

ELVERA: Oh, dear! I didn't know.

OPAL: Now you do, but don't make a big deal out of it.

DORCAS: *(Coming out of the kitchen with plates of dessert.)* *Varsagod. Varsagod.* What were you talking about?

OPAL: Well, if you must know, Dorcas, it was hemorrhoids. Mine've been bleeding lately.

(They eat the desserts.)

ELVERA: Oh, Opal!

DORCAS: Ishda, Opal!

OPAL: Mmm. Isn't this good? Cherry Jello with cherry pie filling.

ELVERA: Who made it?

DORCAS: Opal brought it.

ELVERA: I didn't.

OPAL: I didn't.

DORCAS: *(Confused)* I didn't.

ELVERA: *(Out)* A tasty lunch was served—

OPAL: I think one's thrombosed—is that the word—?

DORCAS & ELVERA: *(Out)* A tasty lunch was served—

DORCAS, ELVERA, & OPAL: *(Out)* A tasty lunch was served—

DORCAS: *(Out)* By hostess Dorcas Briggle—

OPAL: *(Out)* With a new jello dessert that was a gift of Effie Voss.

EFFIE: *(Appears, out)* May 6, 1980.

(DORCAS, ELVERA *and* OPAL *start changing their clothes.*)

WAVA: *(Appears, out)* The Friendly Hour Club met in the home of—

EFFIE: *(Out)* President Effie Voss.

WAVA: *(Out)* There were six members and one guest present—

EFFIE: *(Out)* For the roll call topic: first time driving a car. Elvera Norman?

ELVERA: I hit a man on a horse and the horse had to be put down.

(OPAL *appears with a plant or flowers and sets them where everyone can see.*)

OPAL: That's nothing, I—

ELVERA: Effie, I brought my stamp collection.

EFFIE: Why don't you put it in the boys' old room and we'll look at it later?

(ELVERA *disappears.*)

OPAL: I hit a *team* of horses!

EFFIE: Thank you, Opal Zweifel. Wava Jamtgaard?

WAVA: It was a Model A, I think. That's all I remember. Black and shiny as a crow.

(OPAL *caws.*)

EFFIE: Dorcas Briggle?

DORCAS: *(Appearing)* It *was* a Model A—we learned on the same car. But Pa and Marvin didn't have time to teach me, and you were too nervous, so I just taught myself.

EFFIE: Effie Voss? After the tractor, it was a snap!

OPAL: *(Out)* Lucille was in for hip surgery—

EFFIE: *(Out)* So we voted to give her— Two dollars—

DORCAS: Five dollars—

EFFIE: Five dollars—

DORCAS: Two dollars—

OPAL: *(Out)* Five dollars from the treasury.

ALL: *(Out)* As a get-well gift.

EFFIE: *(Out)* Our guest was Elvera's cousin—

(ALICE *appears with a loaf of bread and a deep voice.*)

ALICE: *(Out)* Alice Bjers.

WAVA: Oh, you brought your famous dark bread Elvera was telling us about!

OPAL: I'd love the recipe.

ALICE: Only if I move, by jinx. Where's Elvera?

EFFIE: I thought she just went to the boys' room, but I bet she went to the kitchen—do you want to— *(Points)*

ALICE: Yes. *(Goes into the kitchen)*

OPAL: She seems nice.

EFFIE: Their farm's on the west side of Beresford.

OPAL & WAVA: *(A bit of disappointment)* Oh.

DORCAS: *(Out)* We talked about our June picnic—

EFFIE: *(Out)* And we decided— *(To the others)* A picnic seems like too much work—

WAVA: I'm not sure I'm up to it, either.

OPAL: Aw, I love the picnic! Palmer does, too.

ALICE: *(Returns and sits down)* Oscar loves picnics.

DORCAS: It's the only time we can get the husbands altogether—

(ALICE suddenly snorts twice and pounds her fist in her crotch a couple of times.)

EFFIE: I'm just not feeling like I could organize—

(ALICE snorts and pounds again.)

OPAL: And they've just done some landscaping at Beresford Park—

(ALICE snorts and pounds.)

EFFIE: Alice, could you give me a little help in the kitchen?

(ALICE and EFFIE go into the kitchen.)

OPAL: *(Out)* —And we decided—

WAVA: *(Out)* —And we decided—

DORCAS & OPAL: *(Out)* —And we decided—

(EFFIE reappears without ALICE.)

EFFIE & WAVA: *(Out)* —And we decided to go to Pizza Ranch instead.

OPAL: Um...what happened to—?

WAVA: Announcement! Announcement! Anniversary!

DORCAS: Oh, Wava.

WAVA: Forty seven years on the ninth of next month, Clarence and Dorcas.

EFFIE: We got to forty-nine.

WAVA: There'll be a party in the church basement, of course—

DORCAS: All the usual nonsense—it's not even an important year—

WAVA: It's important to me. Every anniversary should be.

EFFIE: I agree, Wava. You need to take time to appreciate. Otherwise you only see the faults.

ELVERA: *(Coming in)* Did I hear Alice?

(Silence for a moment)

EFFIE: Alice left.

OPAL: Out the back door?

EFFIE: Probably for her own good.

ELVERA: Did she—? *(Gestures)* She *has* medication, if she'd only take it! *(She runs into the kitchen. In kitchen)* Alice!

(Silence for a moment)

OPAL: Now I'm never gonna get that bread recipe.

(OPAL starts to get up, but has some difficulty. Without a word, WAVA helps OPAL to her feet.)

EFFIE: *(Out)* We drew names for next month's plant exchange.

(OPAL passes around a plastic bag full of slips of paper with their names on them. They each draw names and look at them as they continue talking.)

DORCAS: Opal, are you renting fields to the Huntsmans again this year?

OPAL: Everything except the Buffalo Jump. Palmer never did figure out a way to make it tillable.

EFFIE: No waste like uncultivated land—

WAVA: Mercy, are we all renting our fields out now?

DORCAS: I don't miss swatting grain at all!

EFFIE: Did you hear about the high school play?

WAVA: What?

OPAL: Oh, they had to cancel it, don'tcha know.

DORCAS: Why?

EFFIE: Occult themes. You can bet I made a few phone calls.

DORCAS: What play was it?

EFFIE: Something called *Blithe Spirit*. I don't know what that teacher was thinking.

DORCAS: Effie, you are trying to provoke me—

EFFIE: I am not!

DORCAS: But I refuse to be provoked!

EFFIE: I just thought we should all know what's going on. *(Looking at the plastic bag)* Opal, where did you get this bag?

OPAL: *(Smirking)* From the doctor.

EFFIE: *(Drops the bag)* Opal—heavens!

OPAL: It's clean! It's clean!

WAVA: Mercy! What is it?

DORCAS: *(Examining the bag)* It's a colostomy bag.

OPAL: New—not used!

EFFIE: Not funny, Opal. Not!

(DORCAS giggles.)

OPAL: I wouldn't give you one that I used!

WAVA: Well, as long as it's clean—

IRENE: *(Coming in)* Who was that Elvera's chasing down the road?

ALL: Alice.

EFFIE: She thought she wanted to join the Club but changed her mind.

IRENE: They were both in a lather. What happened?

EFFIE: I have an item I'd like to offer for sale.

DORCAS: It's complicated, Irene.

OPAL: What, Effie?

EFFIE: With the proceeds donated to the hospital. *(Pulls out the violin case)*

DORCAS: Effie, are you sure?

EFFIE: Not like I have need of it.

IRENE: But for—you know—sentimental—

EFFIE: It's just taking up space around the house.

OPAL: Don't any of your kids want it?

EFFIE: None of 'em play, and I can't afford to ship it. What am I bid?

IRENE: I don't play, either.

OPAL: It is a pretty fiddle.

WAVA: I could—

EFFIE: What, Wava?

WAVA: Oh, no—I couldn't possibly—

DORCAS: Wava, go ahead.

WAVA: I could maybe give you five dollars for it.

EFFIE: Five dollars?

DORCAS: I could give ten. Since it's for the hospital.

EFFIE: No, five is fine. Sold! To Wava!

WAVA: *(Taking the violin) Tack sa mycket. (Starts to cry)*

DORCAS: Now, Wava—

IRENE: It's just a violin—

WAVA: I'm sorry, Effie. I don't mean to—

EFFIE: It's all right, Wava—

WAVA: No, it's not! I'm sorry, but I'm mad.

DORCAS: Mad?

EFFIE: At me?

WAVA: Mad at God.

EFFIE: I'm sure he had his—

OPAL: Me, too! You should be, too, Effie!

EFFIE: Now, aside from being blasphemous, it's also useless. We just have to try to see the good in it—

WAVA: *(Gripping the violin case tightly)* There's no good in it, Effie. None! All our lives we hear that God's beni—beno—

DORCAS: Benevolent?

WAVA: Yes! I mean, no! He isn't. He hasn't been benevolent to Effie.

DORCAS: Maybe the good isn't in the things God does.

EFFIE: What does that mean?

DORCAS: Maybe it's in what *we* do.

WAVA: You mean like Effie giving me—

EFFIE: *(Quickly)* Selling!

DORCAS: And God's benevolence is the freedom he gave us—

IRENE: To do good.

OPAL: Or bad.

EFFIE: Dorcas Briggle, you have once again twisted our meeting into irreverence! We're here to have fun, not dwell on bad news and the sinful nature of mankind. Surely someone has something happy to say.

DORCAS: Indeed, Effie, I do, except you'll call it pride.

WAVA: Oh, but it's wonderful, Dorcas! You should be proud. Gwenneth just moved—

EFFIE: Oh, of course, Gwenneth—!

WAVA: Gwenneth got a job in Los Angeles at the Natural History Museum as an orno—ornal—

DORCAS & EFFIE: Ornithologist!

OPAL: But how will you and Clarence stand it with her so far away?

EFFIE: Why, they can go visit, like I visit mine all over the country.

DORCAS: Wouldn't that be nice? But we can't leave Sugar even for a weekend.

EFFIE: Dorcas, don't be silly. I could take that dog for as long as you want. It's the least I can do after you put me in touch with those hospice people from Sioux Falls.

DORCAS: Really, Effie?

EFFIE: You know I love dogs!

IRENE: *(Out)* For the entertainment, Effie showed us her new satellite dish.

(They begin changing clothes.)

WAVA: *(Out)* And we adjourned with a hymn.

DORCAS: Not another hymn!

EFFIE: You're the one who wanted to talk about God!

DORCAS: But not to sing about Him. Her. It!

EFFIE: *(Singing)* Children of the Heavenly Father safely in— *(With special emphasis) His* bosom gather—

(They all join EFFIE in harmonizing the hymn as they change clothes.)

OPAL: *(Out, holding coin purse)* Treasurer's report: old balance—twenty-seven dollars and ninety cents. Dues:

(They each put a quarter in the coin purse.)

OPAL: *(Out)* One dollar twenty-five cents. New balance: twenty-nine dollars and fifteen cents.

WAVA: *(Out)* For our next meeting's craft—

EFFIE: *(Out, with no enthusiasm)* Apple head dolls—

WAVA: *(Out)* Everyone agreed to bring apples and doll clothes.

OPAL: *(Out)* Since it was nice, we sat out on Effie's porch, where—

ALL: *(Out)* A tasty lunch was served.

(The hymn concludes with a final verse.)

WAVA: *(Out)* Our Friendly Hour Club meeting on June 2, 1987—

OPAL: *(Out)* Was held at the new Beresford Library.

EFFIE: This was Dorcas' idea. Where is she?

(OPAL distributes flowers to the others, pinning them on like corsages.)

WAVA: She's coming straight from the hospital.

OPAL: *(Pinning flower on EFFIE)* I thought she was home.

EFFIE: What's this for, Opal?

WAVA: She got out two days ago, but Clarence is still in.

OPAL: I just thought flowers would be nice. Can he talk?

WAVA: Sort of. *Tack sa mycket,* Opal!

OPAL: *Varsagod.*

EFFIE: Wava, what did Dorcas say about Sugar?

WAVA: Oh, Effie—

OPAL: What happened to Sugar?

EFFIE: Nothing, Opal.

WAVA: Effie was taking care of her—

EFFIE: You told her, didn't you?

WAVA: She was still in recovery, and Clarence was in the next room making all kinds of—

EFFIE: Heavens, Wava!

WAVA: I couldn't. I just couldn't!

EFFIE: How can I even face her?

WAVA: Shall we have roll call?

EFFIE: No point in that till more of us are here. Although I move that we send Elvera—

EFFIE & WAVA: *(Out)* A card for her seventy-fourth birthday.

OPAL: She says the Solheim Home doesn't give her all her mail.

EFFIE: Then we can take it to her. *(Looking around)* Aren't we supposed to be getting a tour?

OPAL: Dorcas made the arrangements.

EFFIE: So far this isn't much of a meeting.

OPAL: I have some news.

EFFIE: Opal, none of us want to hear any more about Irene's ashes—

WAVA: Oh! No, I don't!

OPAL: Oh, you won't believe it!

OPAL: She wanted to be under the altar at St. Teresa's—

WAVA: I just don't understand cremation. It doesn't sound restful.

OPAL: But Father Denis wouldn't have it because Bob was an atheist.

WAVA: But wasn't it Irene who wanted to be—

EFFIE: Father Denis is entitled to make his own determination of such things. If Irene wanted to be burnt like a piece of toast, she should have figured on complications.

OPAL: Anyway, that wasn't my news.

(They look at her.)

OPAL: That paleontologist came out from Sioux Falls yesterday. He said there's not a single buffalo at the Buffalo Jump.

EFFIE: There isn't?

WAVA: What's there then?

OPAL: Ice Age mammals. Things with names I can't even pronounce. But they're all fossils, and since they're on my land, I'm allowed to sell 'em.

WAVA: How exciting!

EFFIE: Opal, I'm surprised you let them deceive you like that.

OPAL: Effie, it's true. Mammoths and saber-tooth tigers and things!

EFFIE: Father Denis is going to have atheists crawling all over once those scientists come calling.

(BARB appears. She is a young professional woman in a tailored suit. She has early 80s hair, perhaps with wings.)

BARB: *(Holding out her hand to shake)* Dorcas Briggle?

EFFIE: Oh, no! I'm Effie Voss. President of The Friendly Hour Club.

BARB: Nice to meet you, Effie. I'm Barb Norling. *(To everyone)* And I'll be touring you through the library today. Is this—the whole group?

OPAL: Back in the sixties, there were twice as many of us. The best girls to share lunch with in the whole world. Almost like communion.

EFFIE: Opal, hush, for your own good.

BARB: Is Dorcas here?

EFFIE: Are you the librarian?

WAVA: Dorcas is coming.

OPAL: She had a breast removed a couple of days ago.

EFFIE & WAVA: Opal!

OPAL: And her husband had a stroke at the same time.

BARB: That's awful. Do you want to cancel—?

WAVA: Oh, no, we're here, and Dorcas is on her way. Right, Effie?

EFFIE: You don't look like a librarian.

BARB: I'll take that as a compliment, but I'm a real one, all right, with a Masters in Library Science.

OPAL: Effie majored in Drama, don'tcha know.

EFFIE: You paid good money to learn how to say "shhh"?

BARB: My understanding was that your Club was considering helping us raise money—

(DORCAS *appears but shrinks back from the group, out of sight. She looks distraught, and under the outfit she is wearing, it's obvious she's not yet been fitted for a prosthetic breast.*)

EFFIE: Dorcas was considering that—

BARB: Well, then, before any decisions, can I show you our new facilities?

WAVA: We really should wait for Dorcas—

BARB: We're awfully proud of our community rooms—

EFFIE: Dorcas has seen all this before, I bet.

BARB: I think she has, yes, with one of the assistants—

EFFIE: I'd like to see the children's section.

BARB: *(Leading them off)* It's right over here, and greatly expanded—we're about to go in the "shhh" part of the library—

(As they disappear, DORCAS comes out of her hiding place and catches WAVA, who is looking around for her.)

DORCAS: *(Whisper)* Wava!

WAVA: *(Also whispering)* Mercy! Oh, Dorcas, thank heaven! How are you?

DORCAS: Not so good, Wava.

WAVA: Should I take you home? It's too soon to be out and about—

DORCAS: It's not that—

WAVA: Even so, you ought to be careful. But I'm so glad you're here. Effie's after me to sell her back Walter's violin—

DORCAS: I'll tell her no for you. Find a way to sneak it into my thank-you for taking care of Sugar. But Wava—

(DORCAS takes WAVA's hand for support.)

WAVA: Dorcas, what is it?

DORCAS: Gwenneth was at the hospital today.

WAVA: She's been such a blessing, flying back home to help both—

DORCAS: She's not a blessing, and she didn't help.

WAVA: Dorcas, that's not true! She's been driving and cooking—in her way—!

DORCAS: And talking, Wava. She's been talking. While Clarence can't even say anything except—

WAVA: Cursewords, I know—

DORCAS: She suddenly decided it was time—

WAVA: Maybe she thought he wasn't going to make it—

DORCAS: Or *I'm* not—I don't know—but she told us that she's—

WAVA: Oh, Dorcas—

DORCAS: That she has—

WAVA: I know, Dorcas, I know—

DORCAS: You don't know, Wava, hush up a minute! I've been praying, ever since she was a little girl, that it wasn't so—I can't even say it—

WAVA: You don't have to.

DORCAS: She didn't tell you?

WAVA: No. But sweetie, she's forty-seven years old and she isn't—

DORCAS: Well, neither are you!

WAVA: No, but I'm—

DORCAS: I'm sorry, Wava, that was unkind. I'm not myself. Or maybe I am, and what I am is unkind. I hoped I could just come to The Friendly Hour and everything would be normal again. I need something nice right now—any more bad and I'll go crazy. I thought she just preferred birds to boys. Effie doesn't know, does she?

WAVA: How could she?

DORCAS: She always called Gwenneth a tomboy. Where could this come from? She doesn't have thin lips.

WAVA: Effie's just jealous that Gwenneth is a PhD and none of her kids even finished vo-tech and all moved out-of-state to get away from her. Oh! *(Claps her hand over her mouth.)*

DORCAS: Wava Jamtgaard, that's the meanest thing you've ever said. *(Bursts out laughing)* I'm so proud of you!

(WAVA starts laughing as well.)

DORCAS: That's almost as good as what Clarence said when Gwenneth gave us her news.

WAVA: What was that?

(BARB appears with EFFIE and OPAL.)

DORCAS: Godshit bullfuck!

(DORCAS and WAVA shriek with laughter and collapse into each other's arms tearfully.)

EFFIE: *That's* Dorcas Briggle.

DORCAS: *(Trying to recover quickly)* Oh, Effie, thanks so much for taking care of Sugar again! Her coat is always so shiny when she comes back from your place—sometimes seems like she doesn't want to come home. Could you drop her off later this afternoon?

EFFIE: Dorcas—I—Wava, did you—?

DORCAS: Or if that's inconvenient, I can't pick her up today, but could I come by tomorrow?

EFFIE: Wava—Dorcas—! *(She looks about wildly, then jumps into a closet and slams the door behind her.)*

BARB: Mrs Voss! Mrs Voss? That's not part of our tour. *(To* OPAL*)* It's the custodian's closet!

OPAL: It's all right, Barb, she does this all the time.

BARB: Mrs Voss? Please come out.

OPAL: Wava, what happened to Sugar?

(EFFIE moans from the closet.)

BARB: Excuse me, I'm going to get some help. *(Leaves)*

DORCAS: Wava?

WAVA: Sugar took sick.

DORCAS: She's been sick. She's thirteen.

WAVA: Very sick.

DORCAS: But I gave Effie— *(To the closet)* Effie, you gave Sugar her medicine, didn't you?

WAVA: She did, but Sugar got sicker. Effie had to ask Doctor Wastell to put her to sleep.

(Silence for a moment. DORCAS looks like she's about to explode.)

EFFIE: *(From the closet)* I'm sorry, Dorcas!

DORCAS: Without even asking me?

WAVA: You were in surgery!

DORCAS: Or Clarence?

WAVA: He couldn't even curse at that point!

(DORCAS stands there, stunned.)

EFFIE: *(From the closet)* Is she crying? Dorcas, are you crying? I've been crying ever since.

DORCAS: Effie Voss, you come out of there.

EFFIE: *(From the closet)* No!

DORCAS: If you come out, Wava will consider selling you back Walter's violin.

WAVA: *(Desperate, sotto voce)* Dorcas, no!

EFFIE: You know I can't stand when dogs cry!

DORCAS: Are you coming?

WAVA: Dorcas, you said you'd—!

(The door to the closet swings open. EFFIE stands there with great dignity.)

EFFIE: I'm sorry about Sugar, Dorcas. I loved her like my own.

DORCAS: I know, Effie.

EFFIE: Wava?

WAVA: Dorcas!

EFFIE: I'll understand if you don't want to sell me back that violin—

WAVA: Aren't you going to tell her—?

DORCAS: I will, Wava, I will—

WAVA: Never mind. I'll do it myself. Effie, I still want it. You sold it to me, and I still want it.

EFFIE: I'm the widow—

WAVA: And I'm—well, I don't know what I am, but I want this one thing and I'm sorry but I'm keeping it.

DORCAS: (Out) Our meeting continued at the home of Wava Jamtgaard.

(EFFIE *looks extremely put out. The ladies begin changing clothes.* OPAL *changes into a very nice black or navy dress.*)

WAVA: (Out) With four members present.

OPAL: (Out) Lucille Ostensen was not in attendance, having passed away in May.

EFFIE: (*Trying to recover her dignity, out*) We all did poems about our Club.

OPAL: Here we are girls, once a month we do meet
Be it here or there to our little treat
With that friendly coffee and a bite to eat
Spend an afternoon of relaxing retreat

EFFIE: In May all decided a gift should be bought
Birthday to remember, that special, we thought
Be it June or December we all made the jaunt
We all opened presents—what a happy moment

DORCAS: It goes without saying our Club does have fun
Wava did the serving, fruit salad and bun
Entertainment by Effie, Opal helped, too
Our day was packed full, many things we did do.

WAVA: Mercy! I couldn't possibly rhyme like you
clever girls.

EFFIE: Well, do something, Wava, at least.

DORCAS: Just say what you feel—

WAVA: Like Dorcas said, the day was so full, and now
here we are, looking out on the sunny fields, all of us
together, and you can see—look, do you see? *(Pointing)*
In the west—the clouds—

EFFIE: *(Looking)* Heavens!

WAVA: So many, all banked together, rolling on the
horizon, with the sun behind them, and they look like
mountains, don't they? Like we're not on a flat plain
at all, not an open prairie but in a sheltered valley,
and I like it because you can change where you are
just by thinking, by looking differently, which is silly
but sometimes you just have to. Oh, I'm sorry, I don't
know what I'm talking about.

EFFIE: That wasn't really a poem.

WAVA: Oh, I know—I told you I couldn't—

OPAL: It wasn't even about The Friendly Hour—

DORCAS: I've lived my whole life within four miles of
where I was born, and you just gave me a whole new
way of looking at it.

EFFIE: Well, whatever it was, it was very modern.

OPAL: *(Out, holding coin purse)* Treasurer's report: old
balance—twelve dollars and forty-five cents. Dues:

(They each put a quarter in the coin purse.)

OPAL: *(Out)* One dollar. New balance: thirteen dollars and forty-five cents. *(To the others)* By the way, I did a little math the other day, and calculated that since 1934 The Friendly Hour has made donations totalling—

EFFIE: How much?

OPAL: Three hundred and ninety-four dollars.

EFFIE: That's all?

WAVA: Mercy!

OPAL: *(Proudly)* And served six hundred and eleven lunches to ourselves and others.

EFFIE: *(Out)* There being no further business, old or new—

ALL: *(Out)* A tasty lunch was served.

OPAL: *(Out, isolated from the others)* And the meeting was adjourned.

(Lights out on OPAL in her formal dress.)

EFFIE: *(Out)* Our Friendly Hour Club met on—

DORCAS: *(Out)* July 7, 1992—

(WAVA has flowers that she sets where everyone can see. She no longer has the use of one of her arms.)

WAVA: *(Out)* In the home of—

HAZEL: *(Appears, out)* Hazel Larson. *(She has white hair and a limp.)*

EFFIE: *(Out)* Four members were present for the roll call question:

DORCAS: *(Out)* What is heaven like?

WAVA: Mercy! How could we possibly know?

EFFIE: The Bible tells us.

DORCAS: It isn't very specific.

(DORCAS helps WAVA into a seat.)

EFFIE: It is in Revelations.

HAZEL: Are we sposed to say what it *looks* like?

EFFIE: Ask Dorcas. She picked the question.

DORCAS: What it looks like, what it feels like—

HAZEL: *(Passing out small bowls)* Here, try a little gazpacho. *(Her pronunciation is slightly off.)*

EFFIE: Opal could tell us.

WAVA: Effie, be nice.

DORCAS: Now there's a heaven! Opal passing out chokecherry jelly and knowing everything about everybody—

WAVA: *(Tasting the gazpacho)* Mmm. This is interesting.

EFFIE: Especially now that Palmer's joined her.
(Tasting the gazpacho) Hazel, could you put mine in the microwave? It got a little cold.

HAZEL: It's sposed to be served cold. What *was* Palmer doing in the Flugstad's house at three in the morning?

DORCAS & EFFIE: Julebukking!

HAZEL: What?

WAVA: Oh! Oh, this is spicy!

DORCAS: People used to do that all the time between the holidays around here, but not since the fifties at least.

WAVA: He went a little chrysanthemum after Opal passed. Surprised himself how much he missed her.

EFFIE: The Flugstads thought he was breaking and entering.

DORCAS: One more argument for gun control.

WAVA: Awful, just awful. But a beautiful petunia—I mean—

DORCAS: Funeral?

WAVA: Funeral, yes.

EFFIE: I think heaven's like a big Friendly Hour Club, everyone is friendly and helps each other and there's good food and—

DORCAS: —Opal making people draw Secret Pals from her colostomy bag!

EFFIE: Dorcas Briggle, you're worse than Opal!

(WAVA *laughs*.)

DORCAS: Hazel, what—country—is this from?

HAZEL: Mexico, I'm pretty sure. I think heaven is just being with God. And hell is being without.

DORCAS: I'm not even sure I believe heaven, and I don't believe in hell at all.

EFFIE: You and your books!

HAZEL: By the way, the whole meal has a south of the border theme.

EFFIE: All spicy.

DORCAS: Hell just doesn't seem fair. God wouldn't do that, would he? It seems petty, I guess.

WAVA: I don't think *anyone* goes to heliotrope!

(Silence for a moment)

EFFIE: That's a beautiful idea, Wava, but not the traditional view.

DORCAS: I know what heaven would be for Marvin.

EFFIE: What?

WAVA: Dorcas, no!

DORCAS: *(To* HAZEL*)* He was our brother. When he was in the hospital and on so many painkillers, he thought the room was full of beautiful women who all...

WAVA: Dorcas!

DORCAS: —Wanted him!

WAVA: That is so embarrassing.

EFFIE: Marvin?!

WAVA: It was such a hard time. I don't know how to cook for just myself.

DORCAS & EFFIE: Me, either.

WAVA: Oh, everything's changed! We've changed.

DORCAS: I don't know—when I look at you, or even in the mirror, I still see the girls we were in high school.

WAVA: *(Out)* We'd planned to make clothespin rocking chairs—

EFFIE: *(Out, knowingly)* But everyone forgot clothespins—

DORCAS: *(Out)* So Hazel showed us her latest quilt instead.

WAVA: Ooh, I love white-on-white!

HAZEL: *(Showing the quilt)* It's the hardest, in some ways.

WAVA: But worth it.

DORCAS: I think you should send it to Hillary Clinton.

EFFIE: That'd frost her!

DORCAS: I think she'd like it.

EFFIE: She doesn't like anything regular women do. That's why he always has that look in his eye.

HAZEL: I agree.

WAVA: I'm voting for him. I am.

EFFIE: *(Deliberately changing the subject)* Hazel, your pattern looks like— *(She brings out some lace.)*

WAVA: *(Out)* Effie showed some hardanger lace from her trip to nasturtium.

ALL BUT WAVA: Norway!

EFFIE: I finally went, can you believe it?

HAZEL: Oh, so delicate!

EFFIE: I always wanted to go, and Walter always said we couldn't afford it, so now that I'm on my own, I just did it myself. With Dorcas' help, I mean. *(To DORCAS)* I wish you could have gone.

HAZEL: Why didn't you go?

WAVA: *(Quickly)* Family obligations.

DORCAS: Oh, it was probably more fun to plan than to go.

WAVA: *(Getting up)* Is it time for dues?

EFFIE: Oh, I always forget, without Opal to remind us.

WAVA: Dorcas, can you come with me to get the treasury?

DORCAS: You can't get it yourself? *(Holds out car keys)* Here're the keys.

WAVA: *(Tensely)* I think I need your help.

DORCAS: *(Mystified, but getting up)* Not like it's so heavy it takes two people to carry it.

(DORCAS and WAVA leave out the front door.)

EFFIE: Poor Dorcas.

HAZEL: Why didn't she go with you?

EFFIE: Her daughter Gwenneth had—an accident— well, no, not exactly. Somebody attacked her. Killed her— *(Carefully choosing the word)* —Friend.

HAZEL: Oh!

EFFIE: In Los Angeles. So now's she's back home so Dorcas can take care of her. By herself, now that Clarence's passed. She's got the mind of a child. I don't know how Dorcas does it, seeing as she's practically an atheist.

HAZEL: Do you have to believe in heaven to believe in God?

EFFIE: Can't say that I blame her, with all that's happened. For some people life strengthens faith, for others...Gwenneth was the smartest girl you ever met. An ornithologist.

(EFFIE *does a meadowlark call.* HAZEL *does a bluejay call. They both giggle.* DORCAS *and* WAVA *come back in, also giggling and hiding something.*)

EFFIE: Dorcas, you've got to have faith, for your own good!

DORCAS: What?

(DORCAS *giggles with* WAVA.)

HAZEL: What are you two up to?

(DORCAS *and* WAVA *display a new coin purse with great ceremony.*)

DORCAS & WAVA: Ta-da!

EFFIE: What's that?

DORCAS: A new—

WAVA: I had to get another—

DORCAS & WAVA: Treasury!

EFFIE: What?

HAZEL: Oh, isn't that cute?

EFFIE: What happened to the real one?

WAVA: Oh, Effie, it was split almost in half. I threw it away.

EFFIE: Threw it away?

DORCAS: It was almost sixty years old!

EFFIE: Well, I'm more than sixty years old—do you want to throw me away? What will Opal say?

DORCAS: Um...Effie—

EFFIE: What *would* she say?

WAVA: *(Out, holding coin purse)* Treasurer's report: old balance - nine dollars and twenty cents. Dues:

(They each put a quarter in the new coin purse.)

WAVA: *(Out)* One dollar. New balance: ten dollars and twenty cents.

DORCAS: *(Out)* Effie Voss had the entertainment.

EFFIE: *(Going to the piano)* Let's sing. Something old to remind us of...of things we want to be reminded of.

(EFFIE plays Jeg Er Saa Glad Hver Julekveld and sings it in Norwegian.)

HAZEL: Effie, that's a Christmas—

(DORCAS and WAVA silence HAZEL with a look and start singing along in English.)

HAZEL: Oh, I think I used to know this one, but I can't remember—oh, darnit! *(Hums along)*

(They begin to change their clothes as they sing. The song is slower and quieter than the first time they sang it together.)

DORCAS: *(Out)* We sang old songs for a grand old time.

WAVA: *(Out)* There was no old business and for our new a question was brought up—

(HAZEL proudly produces plates with "South of the Border" cuisine.)

HAZEL: *(Out)* Next time should we go some place for an evening meal?

(WAVA *changes into a dark, formal dress. The plates of food get passed, but no one actually eats. As* HAZEL *changes her clothes, she becomes* ISABELLE.)

WAVA: *(Out)* It was tabled until next meeting.

DORCAS: *(Out)* Wava had made—

EFFIE: *(Out, with great distaste)* Yo-yo crosses—

DORCAS: *(Out)* For each one, which was placed on the table at noon.

WAVA: *(Out)* No further business, meeting adjourned, motion made by—

(DORCAS *puts a bandage around her foot and gets a cane.)*

DORCAS: *(Out)* Dorcas—

WAVA: *(Out)* Seconded by—

EFFIE: *(Out)* Effie—

(DORCAS *and* EFFIE *each end up looking woefully at a plate of spicy food.)*

DORCAS: *(Out, but exchanging a look with* EFFIE *and* WAVA.) And—

EFFIE: *(Out)* And—

WAVA: Hazel, I've never in my life been to Mexico, and I'm too old to go now, but this lovely lunch gave me a whole new experience almost as good as being there. And to think I'd never have tasted *gazpacho* without The Friendly Hour.

DORCAS & EFFIE: A lunch was served—

WAVA: *(Out, isolated from the others)* —And the meeting was adjourned.

(Lights out on WAVA.)

EFFIE: *(Out)* The Friendly Hour Club met at the home of— *(Looks puzzled.)*

DORCAS: *(Out, with a plant)* Dorcas Briggle—

ISABELLE: *(Out, too loud)* On August 3, 1999!

(DORCAS and EFFIE react to ISABELLE's high volume. DORCAS sets the plant where everyone can see.)

EFFIE: *(Out)* With three members present— *(To the others)* That Wava! Always late!

ISABELLE: What?

EFFIE: *(Louder)* Wava is late!

ISABELLE: Oh, no, Effie, she's—

DORCAS: Effie, Wava had another stroke. You remember.

EFFIE: Oh, dear! Of course. When?

DORCAS: A year and a half ago.

EFFIE: Well, then, I apologize. We should send her a dollar.

ISABELLE: *(Too loud)* She's dead!

EFFIE: Oh, then a dollar wouldn't help. Five dollars!

DORCAS: Isabelle, it's so nice you could come back for a visit. Next month will be the sixty-fifth anniversary of our Club!

ISABELLE: No, I'm ninety.

DORCAS: *(Louder)* I meant the Club—

ISABELLE: It's my birthday!

EFFIE: August 3! Isabelle's birthday.

DORCAS: Today?!

ISABELLE: My grand-daughter wants to get me a computer!

(DORCAS and ISABELLE burst out laughing.)

EFFIE: Wava Jamtgaard—October 8. Effie Voss— November 11.

ISABELLE: Oh, but it is good to be back.

EFFIE: Irene Desplinter—December 4.

ISABELLE: I miss the plains—I forget!

EFFIE: Elvera Norman—May 15.

ISABELLE: Colorado is all da mountains.

EFFIE: Lucille Ostensen—July 29.

ISABELLE: Here is safer. You can see what's coming.

EFFIE: Opal Zweifel—June 17.

ISABELLE: What?

EFFIE: *(Louder)* Opal Zweifel—June 17!

ISABELLE: She's dead!

EFFIE: *(After a moment)* That's right. Everybody's dead.

DORCAS: We're not dead, Effie! Isabelle and I are right here.

EFFIE: Where'd our Club go? Something to believe in when everything else lets you down.

DORCAS: It's Isabelle's birthday!

EFFIE: *(Moving to the piano)* Oh!

DORCAS: And we haven't seen her in—

ISABELLE: Twenty-six years!

DORCAS: —How many years?

(EFFIE plays Happy Birthday on the piano, and DORCAS sings along. ISABELLE doesn't hear the song.)

ISABELLE: Dorcas, what happened to your foot?

(EFFIE keeps playing until she finishes the song.)

DORCAS: I was tearing down the corn crib with a new chainsaw, but I guess I wasn't used to it.

ISABELLE: What?

DORCAS: Now you'll have to shoot me.

ISABELLE: What?

DORCAS: I was using a chainsaw—

ISABELLE: What?!

DORCAS: Chainsaw!!

(ISABELLE *adjusts her hearing aid.*)

EFFIE: Where will you put your corn?

DORCAS: Effie, I haven't had corn in years.

EFFIE: What do you feed the pigs?

DORCAS: I don't have pigs, either. I'm not farming at all.

EFFIE: Then what are you doing?

DORCAS: I been wanting to tell you: I got a government grant!

ISABELLE: *(Hearing better now)* What for?

DORCAS: To take out the culverts, fill in the ditches, put in native trees, and plant prairie grass, short and tall.

ISABELLE: You're not doing dat all by yourself?

EFFIE: Sounds like a waste to me.

DORCAS: I'm an old lady, which means I paid Opal's grandkids to do most of it.

ISABELLE: Won't da sloughs fill up?

DORCAS: They already are.

EFFIE: Did they give you a grant to strew boulders in the fields?

ISABELLE: What about da mosquitoes?

DORCAS: The birds eat 'em.

ISABELLE: It just doesn't seem American. Why go to all dat trouble to undo what you did fifty years ago?

DORCAS: Gwenneth likes to watch the birds.

EFFIE: She can't do much else.

DORCAS: It's true.

ISABELLE: Mercy, Effie!

DORCAS: I want her to take some pleasure in life.

EFFIE: Careful with that chainsaw, Dorcas! You coulda cut off your other booby. *(To* ISABELLE, *confidentially)* She had such nice little ones.

ISABELLE: Effie! Heavens!

EFFIE: It's God's judgment.

DORCAS: Maybe we should have a contest.

ISABELLE: What is?

EFFIE: Wouldn't've happened, Dorcas, if you still believed in God.

DORCAS: I do believe in God. It's heaven I don't believe in.

EFFIE: But you *have* to believe in hell.

DORCAS: I couldn't possibly.

EFFIE: How can you believe in God and not believe in hell? That's the whole reason for believing in God! We'll see him face to face when we die.

DORCAS: Effie, I still pray—I do. And God answers.

EFFIE: By taking away—

DORCAS: When Gwenneth was little, I prayed. I worried and I prayed. I could see she was—

EFFIE: A tomboy.

DORCAS: Yes. And when she grew up and—

EFFIE: Never married.

DORCAS: I prayed more. I feared for her. And then my fears came true—she told me and Clarence...about her friend in Los Angeles. So I prayed for a change.

EFFIE: They can change if they want.

DORCAS: Gwenneth told me she never would. I couldn't accept it. I prayed harder for change. Then— the—attack—the worst thing possible for a child, for *my* child. I brought Gwenneth home. I prayed some more. And a miracle occurred: God changed *me.*

(Silence for a moment)

ISABELLE: A contest sure sounds nice!

EFFIE: Or a game! Bunko!

DORCAS: All right—

EFFIE: No, King's Corner!

ISABELLE: Carom!

EFFIE: Remember that time Opal's kids stole the jelly beans right out from under her chair?

ISABELLE: No prizes that day!

DORCAS: *(Out)* We discussed games and contests—

EFFIE: Bowling!

ISABELLE: *(Out)* But decided not to play.

EFFIE: Hearts!

(The ladies begin changing clothes.)

DORCAS: *(Out)* Dorcas Briggle made a special cake—

ISABELLE: *(Out)* For Isabelle's ninetieth.

(ISABELLE changes into a dark formal dress. EFFIE changes into a housecoat.)

EFFIE: *(Out)* She blew out all the candles on the cake—

ALL: *(Out)* Not ninety!

EFFIE: *(Out)* There being no new business—

DORCAS: *(Out)* And no old business—

ISABELLE: *(Out)* A motion for adjournment was made—

(While changing, DORCAS *is for a moment topless, and looks at her breasts in the mirror.)*

DORCAS: *(Out)* And seconded.

ALL: *(Out)* Motion carried.

ISABELLE: *(Out, isolated)* The meeting was adjourned.

(Lights out on ISABELLE.*)*

DORCAS & EFFIE: *(Out)* And a tasty lunch was served.

(Lights out on EFFIE. DORCAS *gets a cane and a brown paper shopping bag.)*

DORCAS: *(Out)* Our Friendly Hour Club met— *(Pause)* On September 4, 2007— *(Pause)* At the Bethesda Home— *(Pause)* With two members in attendance.

*(*DORCAS *enters a private room in a retirement home.)*

DORCAS: Effie? *(As there is no response, she sets down her shopping bag and takes out a plant, setting it where everyone can see. She looks outside.)* Effie? *(She returns to the room and sits down. Out)* The roll call question was "blessings." Dorcas Briggle? Oh, there are so many! But today I would say The Friendly Hour. Effie Voss? *(No response)* Opal Zweifel? *(Slightly imitative of* OPAL.*)* My crisp, green pickles! They never let me down, don'tcha know. *(Her own voice)* Isabelle Hagen? *(Loud) Jag maste saga att det ar min symaskin.* [I'd have to say my sewing machine.]

(Intrigued, EFFIE *starts peeking out of the closet.* DORCAS *pretends not to see her.)*

DORCAS: *(Her own voice)* Irene Desplinter? *(*IRENE's *western accent)* Blackie at a trot across a snowy field. *(Her own voice)* Elvera Norman? *(*ELVERA's *voice)* My stamp collection, no, my ant farm—rocks! Oh, I can't decide! *(Her own voice)* Lucille Ostensen? *(Silence)* Lucille?

EFFIE: Plants.

DORCAS: Oh, hello, Effie. I brought you one.

(EFFIE *looks confused.*)

DORCAS: A plant. *(Shows her)*

EFFIE: *Tack sa mycket.*

DORCAS: *(Out)* We talked about craft projects over the years.

(DORCAS *takes out the gold egg-carton Easter decoration.*)

EFFIE: *(Truly enraptured)* Beautiful! *(Places it somewhere, with ceremony)*

DORCAS: *(Out)* And approved the minutes.

(DORCAS *takes out a few old notebooks and gives them to* EFFIE.*)*

DORCAS: Effie, do you realize we've never once approved the minutes?

EFFIE: Never?

DORCAS: In all these years!

EFFIE: We're out of order!

DORCAS: I move for acceptance of the minutes.

EFFIE: *All* the minutes?

DORCAS: Do I have a second?

EFFIE: Second!

DORCAS: *(Putting her hand on the minutes)* Discussion?

EFFIE: *(Putting her hand on the minutes)* Nineteen thirty-four. And now it's nineteen—

DORCAS: Two thousand—and seven!

EFFIE: Heavens, we're old!

DORCAS: All those in favor?

DORCAS & EFFIE: Aye!

EFFIE: *(Delighted)* Motion carries!

DORCAS: Effie, I got permission to take you for a drive.

EFFIE: Permission?

DORCAS: I want to show you something.

EFFIE: I don't need permission.

DORCAS: Then let's go.

(With a lighting change and sound effect, their chairs become the car interior. EFFIE looks out the window as DORCAS drives.)

DORCAS: That was Saugstads. It's an Amish family now.

EFFIE: Amish!

DORCAS: They home-school the kids.

EFFIE: They should go to college. *(Looking)* Oh! The Buffalo Jump!

DORCAS: Opal sold it to the government. It's a national monument now.

EFFIE: *(Reading, disapproving)* Buffalo Jump Fossil Beds. She was always shrewd. *(Looking, concerned)* Where's the Legion Hall?!

DORCAS: Torn down in '74. But there's a new one on the west side of town. *(Turning the car)* Here we are.

EFFIE: Where?

DORCAS: *(Out)* We visited the home of Dorcas Briggle.

EFFIE: It isn't!

DORCAS: *(Pointing)* The house is just the same.

EFFIE: Heavens! Where's the barn?

(Lighting change as DORCAS helps EFFIE out of the car and they walk.)

EFFIE: The tractor shed? The fields?

(The lighting illuminates the plants set out earlier.)

DORCAS: These are my fields now.

EFFIE: It's all weeds!

DORCAS: *(Pointing)* Big bluestem, Indian grass, Canada wild rye, switchgrass—that's tall grass that I seeded. *(Pointing elsewhere)* Short grass: little bluestem, side-oats grama, hairy grama, prairie drop seed—and then some flowers mixed in: Purple cone flower, New England aster, common milkweed—that attracts monarch butterflies—and ashy sunflower.

(No reaction from EFFIE.*)*

DORCAS: I put in some trees—burr oak, mostly. And look—sloughs, more than before, full of ducks!

EFFIE: *(After a moment)* What would Clarence say after all his work? You might as well set it all on fire and start over.

DORCAS: I do! Opal's boys start controlled burns, I think they call it.

*(*EFFIE *just shakes her head at the waste.)*

DORCAS: Oh, I have something for you. *(Moves a chair)* Sit down.

*(*EFFIE *sits, glowering.* DORCAS *leaves. After a moment,* ISABELLE *appears and makes her mourning dove sound.* EFFIE *reacts, and* ISABELLE *disappears.* WAVA *appears and does her loon call, then disappears.* OPAL *appears, does a crow call, and disappears.* DORCAS *reappears carrying a shopping bag in one hand and Walter's violin case in the other.* DORCAS *quacks.* EFFIE *turns toward her.)*

DORCAS: Wava thought you might want— *(She holds out the violin.)* I keep forgetting—

EFFIE: *(Taking the violin, tears in her eyes)* Oh! *(She hugs it.)* Oh!

DORCAS: Effie, I'm sorry, maybe I shouldn't—

EFFIE: *(Looking at* DORCAS*)* I see Him!

DORCAS: Who? Walter?

EFFIE: No, God! Heavens!

DORCAS: You see God? Effie, you're not—

EFFIE: Right in front of me! Face to face!

DORCAS: Are you all right? Should I call the doctor?

EFFIE: *(Touching* DORCAS*)* You!

DORCAS: What?

EFFIE: I didn't answer roll call.

DORCAS: That's okay, I know you're here.

EFFIE: Blessings. For roll call. You.

DORCAS: Me?

EFFIE: You're my blessing.

*(*IRENE *appears, does her hawk cry, then disappears.* WAVA *appears, wails like a loon, and disappears.* OPAL *caws and disappears.)*

EFFIE: I'm so happy to have this. I only wish...

DORCAS: What?

EFFIE: I wish...I knew why I wanted it!

DORCAS: *(Out)* Treasury report: thirteen dollars and seventy-five cents.

EFFIE: Oh, very good.

DORCAS: Effie, I'm thinking this is maybe our last meeting of The Friend Hour.

EFFIE: Oh, no!

DORCAS: What do you think?

EFFIE: Well...I guess we will have to end Club since it's so hard for anyone to have it now.

DORCAS: *(Indicating treasury)* And what shall we do with this? Do you want to split it?

EFFIE: Let's give it...to the library!

DORCAS: So moved.

EFFIE: *(Digging in her pocket)* Second. Here's a quarter to bring it to an even fourteen.

DORCAS: *(Digging in her purse)* And here's another dollar to make it fifteen. Those in favor?

DORCAS & EFFIE: *(Sadly)* Aye.

DORCAS: I brought a little lunch. *(She takes out some food.)*

EFFIE: Not hungry. Not.

DORCAS: You have to eat. For your own good.

(WAVA's loon and OPAL's crow can be heard. EFFIE makes a meadowlark call, in response. DORCAS starts to feed EFFIE.)

EFFIE: I can do it myself!

DORCAS: Sorry!

(EFFIE starts to eat. DORCAS quacks. OPAL crows.)

DORCAS: *(Looking around)* I know the farm's not what it was, Effie. Nothing is.

EFFIE: All changed!

DORCAS: But maybe for the better.

EFFIE: Like we were never here.

(WAVA wails. LUCILLE appears, does the sloughpumper sound, disappears. OPAL crows. DORCAS listens as she thinks about what EFFIE has said.)

DORCAS: How's your lunch?

EFFIE: *(With great appreciation)* Tasty!

(IRENE cries. EFFIE responds with the meadowlark song. DORCAS quacks. LUCILLE does the sloughpumper. ISABELLE

does the mourning dove. OPAL *crows.* HAZEL *does the*
bluejay. IRENE *does the hawk.* WAVA *wails. The bird sounds*
weave into beautiful cacophony.)

END OF PLAY

www.ingramcontent.com/pod-product-compliance
Lightning Source LLC
Chambersburg PA
CBHW052123090426
42741CB00009B/1925